Cedar Island
Duck Hunting Experiences

HORACE O. KELLY, JR.

Cedar Island Duck Hunting Experiences
ISBN: 978-0-9987146-2-2
Copyright © 1990 Horace O. Kelly, Jr.
Republished 2018 by Dr. Lora Kelly Shahine, the author's daughter
All Rights Reserved.

Preface: A Note on the Republication of Cedar Island Duck Hunting Experiences

By Lora Shahine, MD
the Author's Daughter

    I am honored to have the opportunity to republish my father's book, Cedar Island Duck Hunting Experiences. My father had a passion for hunting and spent over 20 years duck hunting on Cedar Island, NC, a small, charming community of hard-working people. He cherished these trips—the anticipation, the people he grew to know and love, the scenery and nature. Year after year, stories and memories built up, and he wrote them down in this collection of humorous tales and poignant memories for all to enjoy.

    My father died of a sudden heart attack at age 57 but accomplished a great deal in his time on this earth. An entrepreneur, a professor, a husband, a father, and an avid golfer and hunter, he lived life to the fullest and left his influence on anyone fortunate enough to know him. I remember him writing this book and self-publishing it in the 1990s. He was passionate about recording his experiences, and the final book was well received by everyone who read it.

    I read this book every few years and laugh at the silly stories and reflect on the subtle lessons learned in between them. Each story is unique. I love the jokes, laughs, and stories of camaraderie among the hunters and guides. I am touched by how he writes about my mother's strength and resilience in "The Lady Duck Hunter." I am deeply moved by his account of the loss of a young man on the island to AIDS in the late 1980s in "Edward and Gerald Wain Gaskill, Jr." Although we've come a long way in our understanding of HIV and AIDS, this story happened in the beginning, when

AIDS was full of shame and guilt. This community of 250 hard-working fishermen and women surrounded one of their own with love and understanding and supported the family through loss, and I can only now truly understand what that meant.

I had the pleasure of duck hunting with my father once before he died, and it is one of my fondest memories of him. I cherish the memories of sitting in the duck blind with him, eating those Wrangler hot dogs he loved so much, and being with him in one of his favorite places. As a mother now, I can appreciate how much he must have loved sharing this experience with me—watching me down my first duck and bust out of the duck blind to retrieve it.

Although hunting is not one of my own passions now, the memories of him will last forever, and I'm thrilled to share this book with you. Here is Cedar Island Duck Hunting Experiences, by Horace O. Kelly, Jr.

Enjoy!

Lora Shahine, MD
November 2018

Dedication

This little book of stories is dedicated to several people.

To those wonderful people who live and work at Cedar Island—if it were not for them, none of this would have been possible.

To my friends and family who have enjoyed these experiences with me as we look forward to many more great times at the island.

And finally, to those who might read this book who have never been. Part of your life is missing, and after reading this book, you know where you can find that missing pleasure and enjoyment.

Happy Reading!

Horace O. Kelly, Jr.
February 1990

Table of Contents

Preface 2
Dedication 4
Introduction 7
In the Beginning... 8
The First Trip 12
James and His Famous Biscuits 23
Newt and His Blowout 24
The Famous Cedar Island Buffleheads; AKA Buffalo Brains; AKA Dippers 26
The Frozen Shotgun 28
The Charlie Maddry 'Stomp' 30
He Div!—He Div Again! 32
Famous Last Words—"You Can Wade Here!" 37
Those Pintails Had on Oxygen Masks 40
Have-a-Lock, Have-a-Lock, Have-a-Lock Today! 43
Red Drawers Flapping in the Breeze 45
Just Keep Going—You Can Make It 47
Don't Worry—It's Only Your Waders That Are on Fire! 50
The Lady Duck Hunter 53
Does It Ever Get Cold at Cedar Island? 56
Can One Be Comfortable With His Waders Filled With Water? 58
Down Here, We Call That a "SHELLDRAKE" 61
It's Another World—And Another Language 64
John and His First Goose 66
Watch Out for the Sand Sharks When Retrieving Your Ducks! 68
If You Don't Sit Down and Shut Up, I'll Leave You Here All Night! 71
That SOB Just Left Me a Rusty Shotgun 74
A Most Unexpected Gift 76
Even Ira Paul Can Get Flustered and Speechless Occasionally . . 78
Edward and Gerald Wain Gaskill, Jr 83

The Dedicated Guide	89
Traditions	91
But I Thought That Was a Legitimate Duck!	95
Do Sea Gulls Like Alka-Seltzer?	99
Floating Seats and Other Duck Blind Discomforts	101
The Stalk	103
If You Have a Dog, Leave Him at Home!	108
Stand-Uppers Are Okay—As Long as You Are Not One of Them	111
Jerry's Infamous Lunches	113
The Unplugged Gun	115
John Said, "Boy, This Is Like Shooting Sitting Ducks"	119
A Nice, Unexpected Touch	122
Watch Out for a Case of "Crack-Eye"	124
Nasal-Wik-a-Ways	126
Charlene's First Shot	128
Fetch	131
Horace, Do You Like Clams?	134
Would You Like to Take Home a Few Oysters?	136
Cedar Island Guides Are a Hardy Bunch	138
If You Need a Kidney Workout, go to Cedar Island	141
At Cedar Island, Sharp Curves Mean SHARP CURVES	143
Game Wardens Have Their Ways	145
Other Sights and Sounds to Keep You Awake	147
If You Don't Grab That Wand—Boy, It Will Kill You!	148
A Breeding Ground for Commerce	151
M R Duks	154
Christmas at Cedar Island	156
The Exploding Beanee Weanees	158
There Is More to Cedar Island Than Just Killing Ducks	160
About the Author	163
About the Republication	164

Introduction

Life, as wiser people than I have observed, is a struggle of ups and downs and usually more downs than ups. I suppose it is how you handle the downs that makes life enjoyable or not so enjoyable. I have also found that if you have something to look forward to, no matter how little or insignificant it may seem at the moment, those "things to look forward to" are the vehicles to help you up and over the valleys that all of us encounter.

Cedar Island duck hunting, for the past 13 years, has been one of those vehicles that has helped me more than I can say. This past season, while sitting in a duck blind with my good friend and hunting partner Charles Maddry, Charlie suggested that I put these experiences down for memory's sake. We felt that if no one but the two of us enjoyed them, the writing would be worth the effort. There is no rhyme or reason to the order of these "little stories," except as my own memory dictates. For that reason, I shall just call them "experiences," for want of a better word.

In the Beginning...

In the early seventies, Jerry Gaskill, manager and part owner of Driftwood Enterprises, conceived the idea of staging duck and goose hunting out of his motel at Cedar Island. It began rather inauspiciously as Jerry contracted with four commercial fishermen to serve as guides. It was ideal for these men since they could not normally fish during early December and January, and this provided them with an additional source of income during the bitter winter months on the bays and sounds around Cedar Island. These stalwart four were James Goodwin, Dallas Goodwin (cousins—everybody at Cedar Island is related to each other in one way or the other), Ira Paul Day, and Clyde Thomas Styron. I mention their names not for any recognition value, but because I will refer to them from time to time, and if you have become acquainted with them, the stories will be a lot more meaningful.

All of these men are the type of strapping, marvelous specimens of manhood that only spending 14 to 16 hours a day as watermen can produce. Yet each has his own eccentricities and deserves individual mention.

James Goodwin, who is in his mid-forties and married to Rachel, has two sons, one of whom plans to follow in his father's footsteps and be a fisherman. James has little education but is wise in "water ways" like few I have known. "Huckleberry," as he is known to his friends, is always ready with a willing smile, has a shock of red hair that is always covered with a cap that sits at almost right angles to his head, and is famous for building his own boats, from which he works. I have gotten to know James pretty well over the years since he was the first guide to whom I was assigned, and I stayed with James for about seven to eight years until he decided he could make more money "clamming" during the duck season.

When James decided to hang up his guiding hat, I specifically asked for Dallas Goodwin. Dallas, James' cousin, is a huge man—about six feet six inches—and his hands are about the size of a 250-count clam sack. I was always afraid to shake hands with Dallas for fear of never being able to use mine again; however, he surprised me when I first did shake hands with him—he seemed to try not to shake hands too hard—maybe he had broken so many hands in his day that he learned that we white collar types could not match his hearty "downeast" greeting. Despite his imposing size and obvious ability to overpower anything or anyone who might stand in his way, I have found Dallas to be one of the gentlest and most caring human beings I have ever met. Dallas always seemed to try very hard to put us in blinds where he felt we would get the best shooting.

Dallas has now decided to fish instead of guide, and I think we have a new guide who will fill James' and Dallas' shoes just fine. He is Howard Gaskill—remember, I told you everybody is related. One distinguishing characteristic I can say about Howard; besides being a good guide and a very hard worker, he can put away more food at one sitting than any other human I know.

One evening, we had a buffet dinner, and Howard ate with me and my hunting partner, Charles Maddry. Now Charles can put it away, but he looked like an anemic hospital patient compared to Howard's many refills. About 45 minutes after Charlie and I had finished, Howard put down his fork and announced he had to "go grab a snack before going to bed." As Charlie and I walked to the room, we wondered out loud whether Howard ever got any dinner invitations to the homes on the island.

Many of the guides at Cedar Island have rightfully been accused of being "water taxis" as they take their clients out to a blind at the beginning of the day but never offer to move them, even if they know that good shooting can be had at some other location.

Dallas was never hesitant to pick us up and move us, even though there was a lot of effort in doing so. Forty to sixty decoys must be picked up and then replaced in another location, not to speak of the time, trouble, and gasoline expense of moving a couple of hunters.

I never had the pleasure of hunting with Ira Day or Clyde Styron, even though I got to know them rather well. Ira was the joker of the group and could tell the tallest tales of anyone. Ira is fine today, but we were all saddened when we learned that he had contracted a debilitating disease (Guillain-Barré) that left him partially paralyzed and unable to fish or guide. He was bedridden for most of two years, but I am happy to say that he is back fishing again and doing well.

Clyde Styron comes from a long family of east coast Styrons, and you will find his family in the history books on Cedar Island, Portsmouth, and Ocracoke Islands as settlers and fishermen as far back as the history books go. Clyde is the slightest of build of the four, but an excellent fisherman and guide. He, like Dallas, always seems to want his hunters to do well.

Clyde is also the crew-appointed mechanic, and anytime there was motor trouble, which was often considering the shallowness of the bays and sounds around Cedar Island and the "hell-bent for leather" approach these guides take in getting you to your appointed blind, Clyde was always the man to find and fix any problem that arose.

Jerry Gaskill is the brains behind the Cedar Island operation. Jerry is a short, stocky, graying late-forties man of boundless energy. Jerry is the most outgoing and friendliest man I have ever met, and to meet him, you would never know that he had suffered any tragedies in his life.

When you ask Jerry, "How are you doing?," he will inevitably reply "Finest kind!" or "Doing great!," and he means it. Jerry has two sons: Clay, who is about 23 and divides his time between running the gas dock, selling fuel and supplies to local fishermen, and quickly becoming one of the newest fishermen on the island, and David, a blond 14-year-old who has just acquired his own boat and has already started to think about becoming a fisherman.

Jerry's wife is Charran, and she has become as indispensable to Jerry as anything in his life. Jerry and Charran have only been married for four years as of this writing, and she has stood beside him through two major family tragedies. Without her, I am not sure Jerry would have made it. They have built a beautiful home together and have become two of our dearest friends.

Well, now to the stories.

The First Trip

I first learned about Cedar Island duck hunting from a friend of mine at R.J. Reynolds. Jimmy Walker and his father had gone, and Jimmy came back with tall tales about "clouds of ducks" everywhere and shooting until his barrel glowed at Cedar Island. This was enough for me—it sounded like something that I needed to try.

I had been going hunting with Charlie Maddry to Nantahala for bear and boar; and one thing you have got to remember is that Charlie is a "professional hunter." Since I was really a novice hunter anyway, and besides that I had never been duck hunting, I did not think it was appropriate to invite Charles to go to the coast with me until I had checked it out first hand. After all, I did not want to be embarrassed. I have learned something about myself in my 51 years and that is, I want to do it first myself and learn the ropes before I submit my friends to the experience.

Since this would be my first experience at Cedar Island hunting, and a game I have never hunted before, who better to ask to go along than my wife, who had never even fired a gun? There was no way that I would be embarrassed with someone who was more of a novice than I was.

We had received a map from Jerry that would take us straight to the Driftwood Motel, our home away from home for the duck hunting experience. We packed all the clothes we could find because Jimmy had said that we sat in a box for 12 hours and it was cold as hell!

Cedar Island is about 35 miles northeast of Morehead City, North Carolina, and I had been to Morehead City before, so it did not seem to be an arduous drive. We decided to leave about noon (our first mistake) so as to have plenty of time to arrive at the motel and get situated. An ominous sign—it began to rain as we left Winston-Salem for our first trek to the coast in search of the elusive Atlantic coast flyway waterfowl.

The trip was uneventful—by that I mean no major mishaps the first four hours. Four hours from Winston-Salem will put you in front of Neuse Sporting Goods in Kinston, North Carolina. Anyone coming from the western part of the state going anywhere near Morehead City must travel US 70, which takes you through Kinston and right in front of Neuse. It is impossible for a hunter or fisherman to bypass Neuse Sporting Goods. It is the only sporting goods store I know of that stays open 24 hours a day, 365 days a year (at least that used to be the case).

Since that trip, part of the "tradition" of going to the coast to hunt with Jerry Gaskill and the Driftwood Doughboys is stopping at Neuse. You don't have to buy anything (although we always do)—just stopping there and looking at all the goodies is all that is required. Also, a pretty good lunch can be had next door at King's Restaurant if you like real southern home cooked barbecue, collard greens, pinto beans, etc. Nowadays, we time our trips to take in Neuse and King's—if we didn't, we probably would not see a duck the whole time we were there (at least that is the unspoken feeling we have).

We continued on through Morehead City, bypassing Tony's Sanitary Seafood Market (a marvelous place to eat despite what the name might conjure up in your imagination). We would like to have stopped at Tony's; however, it was getting toward sundown, and I wanted to be at the motel before dark (that turned out to be a joke on us). Yes, I said it was only 35 miles or so to Cedar Island from Morehead City; however, that is the longest 35 miles in the history of map making. You must traverse many "small" coastal towns on unlit highways, through marshlands with water canals on each side of the road, and it is impossible to go over 40 miles an hour because of the twists and turns.

    Jerry's map clearly said take Highway 70 directly to the motel, and that is what we aspired to do. About 12 miles from the motel, Highway 70 bears off to the right toward a fishing village called Sea Level. Not knowing the area, we assumed that the Driftwood Motel must be at Sea Level, so we took the turn off and headed into the town. By now, it was raining again, and because of the twisting, turning road from Morehead City, it was also dark. Sea Level is small by anyone's standards, and there was only one motel/hotel in town, and it was clearly not the Driftwood. Charlene, my wife, is one of those people who tends to keep fears well hidden and not discussed. By now, after some six hours in the rain and with darkness upon us and us lost, she was "very quiet."

    After about 30 minutes of searching (and you can search the entire town of Sea Level in less than five minutes), we retraced our steps back to the highway where we had taken the turn into Sea Level. At the junction, we noticed that Highway 12 continued on east, and the only other choice was to return toward Morehead City—and we knew that could not be the correct direction. Therefore, we took Highway 12 and headed off east toward an unknown destination.

    If you have never been on N.C. Highway 12 after dark in the pouring down rain, not knowing where you were going, you have an unenviable experience ahead of you. There are no street lights—there is no "white line" in the highway—there are no road signs—there is no inhabited life (wild or otherwise) in sight—just a never ending dark road going heaven knows where. That is the way we felt that night, and we began to joke about being lost—"whistling in the graveyard" I believe they call it.

Today, Highway 12 is slightly more inhabited than it was on that December night in 1976, but it is still an eerie drive that I never look forward to.

What a relief to finally come around a bend and see the Driftwood Motel in all its splendor. The motel is at the Cedar Island end of the Cedar Island Ocracoke ferry run, and although it is not the end of the world, "you can see it" from the motel. The motel was built around the late 1950s with few amenities, since it is mostly inhabited by travellers who have either missed the ferry from Ocracoke and must wait until the morning run or by those who got seasick on the crossing and cannot face the drive to Morehead City. It possesses few of the comforts of home. In fact, there are no telephones in the rooms, and the television only receives three stations. Nevertheless, it has become one of the most welcome sights you can imagine after a day of facing the wind and cold from a duck blind.

In the summer, the motel remains fairly well occupied with vacationers and fishermen who come to Cedar Island to fish the waters of Pamlico Sound and the bays and sounds around the island.

Since this was our first trip, we had a lot to learn. We checked into the motel and were given a typewritten sheet of rules and regulations and an alarm clock and told that breakfast was at 5:15 am. We unloaded our car and stashed our belongings in the room and headed over to dinner.

Dinner was the beginning of our many pleasant surprises at Cedar Island. The food is magnificent. The seafood is fresh each day and the crab cocktails are an epicurean's delight. Everything prepared in the restaurant is top drawer except the "CoreSound Clam Chowder," which is made with water instead of milk or tomato sauce. Not to be missed is the lemon meringue pie.

This leads me to introduce Marcel, Jerry's sister, who makes the lemon pies and now supervises the kitchen chores for the motel. When we first began coming to Cedar Island, the kitchen was "manned" by Katy.

Katy is a seemingly crotchety old lady who is now about 75 and still going strong. She was married to a fisherman and has, over the years, learned to not take anything off anybody. This "crotchetiness" is all surface—down deep she is as lovable and nice as all the other Cedar Island folk.

Katy used to make the announcements every morning about how the hunters were supposed to sign their lunch checks and leave them at the front desk before going to their rooms to finish dressing for the day's hunt. A Cedar Island accent requires a finely tuned ear, and Katy's was "stronger" than anybody's except Jerry Gaskill's and Ira Paul Day's. No one ever fully understood what Katy was saying anyway, but one morning, after serving pancakes the day before (which everyone was still full from), Katy made her customary morning announcements. However, this morning she made the mistake of asking the hunters if they would like pancakes again the next morning. The groans and moans could be heard in the parking lot, and Katy uttered some untranslatable comments and stormed off to the kitchen. Needless to say, breakfast the next morning was no culinary delight, and we all learned that we had best stay on the good side of Katy or suffer the consequences.

At dinner, the guides come by your table and introduce themselves and tell you to be at the boat dock at 6:00 am to load up and go out to the blinds. They chit chat for a while, doing their public duty, which is quite foreign to them. One of the phrases that you quickly learn at Cedar Island is, "I don't know what to tell you, Horace!" This is an appropriate phrase for any number of questions, such as,

"How is the hunting?"; "Which way will they likely fly tomorrow"; "Will we hunt the banks or the marshes?"; "What kind of duck is this I just shot?"—the list of questions is endless, but the answer is always the same. I used to suppose this prevented the guides from committing themselves to any "truths," but after years of hunting at Cedar Island, I have come to believe that there are, in fact, no absolutes or truths to be known.

Each day is a new adventure, and the guides are quite truthful in saying, "I don't know what to tell you, Horace!"

Katy still works in the kitchen, but Marcel now directs everything and is probably the best cook "I have ever eaten after except Charlene." Marcel and I have become pretty good friends, and every time I come down, she is alerted by Jerry and always prepares enough lemon pies so not only can I have a piece at dinner, but usually have a whole pie ready for me to take home when I leave.

Also, Cedar Island serves the best bacon and sausage I have ever eaten (although my doctor doesn't think that I partake of these types of goodies anymore). Marcel usually has several pounds of bacon and sausage wrapped up for us and has been known to throw in a dozen soft shell crabs and other delicacies for us to enjoy when we get back home. She is the jewel in the Cedar Island crown.

After dinner, we went back to the room determined to get some sleep before the alarm went off at 4:30 am. It is difficult to sleep when there are hunters blowing duck calls in the parking lot and playing cards in the next room until the wee hours of the morning. This is usually solved by the second day because you are so exhausted at the end of the first day's hunt that anything other than sleep is out of the question.

The problem is that there are always first time hunters coming in every night who must practice their duck calls. If you hunt at Cedar Island very often, you soon realize that two things are absolutely useless on waterfowl hunts over bays and sounds like Cedar Island—and they are duck calls and retrievers. Birds simply do not respond to calls over such wide expanses of water, and I will write more later about the uselessness of dogs in this type of waterfowl hunting.

The next morning came very soon, but, like the troopers we were, we trudged, partially dressed, to the dining room. We quickly learned that if you position yourself properly (that is, where you can see the kitchen), you can be the first in line for breakfast. Now there is an excellent reason for this.

After breakfast, you must get dressed—not an easy task considering all you have to put on—and you have to get to the boat dock on time or suffer the wrath of the other hunters. If you want to have any time to visit the potty one last time before putting on your 40 pounds of down and thinsulate, you had better be first in the breakfast line so you can eat and get out of there in a hurry and give yourself a few more minutes in your room. If you have ever tried to take a crap in a four by six foot box over three feet of water with the wind howling around your arse, you can appreciate the judicious position in the dining room for breakfast.

After eating, you grab your pre-prepared lunch and head to the room to finish dressing. After last minute packing, we are in the car and headed for the boat dock.

James brings his flat-bottomed skiff up to the dock, and we load our gear in and settle down under his "house" for the trip to the Outer Banks. Another tip you quickly learn is to grab a life jacket, not for the obvious reasons most people grab life jackets, but to use as a cushion to sit on. If you have ever ridden in a flat-bottomed skiff in three to four foot seas sitting on a hard bench and bouncing up and occasionally banging your head on top of the "house," you can appreciate the necessity of the life jacket.

A word of explanation about the "houses" on these boats. These are converted fishing boats that are about 22 feet long and about eight feet wide with completely open cockpits. They are powered by 150 to 200hp outboard motors, and the steering mechanism is an upright stick in the center of the boat with ropes going from the steering stick down the sides of the boat and attached to the motor. The waterman stands as he drives the boat, and it is open for the purpose of loading fish during the fishing season.

When duck hunting comes around, the guides build shelters over the front of the boat up to the steering stick so hunters can be sheltered from foul weather. They also build small seats along the sides of the boat for hunters to sit on. This leaves little clearance between the hunters' heads and the top of the "house." Hence the need for the life jacket to sit on.

The ride to the blind is an awesome experience. It is pitch dark, and somehow the guides know just which channel to follow and how to navigate around the marshes to avoid running aground. After about 30 minutes, the guide will tell you to hold on, and shortly after that, the motor is bumping the bottom because we are in shallow water at the first blind. Two hunters unfold themselves and climb into their blind while the guide tosses out decoys. Good wishes are given to the two departed hunters, and we are off to the next blind. Long before sunrise, all six hunters are placed in their blinds, and the guide is off to do whatever it is guides do until mid-morning when they return to check on you.

The first order of business is to stow our gear in appropriate places in the blind, load the guns, and settle back, hoping for the sound of wingbeats or the splashes of ducks landing in our decoy spread.

As the sun comes up, the scenery is breathtaking. As far as the eye can see is water, and about a mile away are the Outer Banks of North Carolina, and the sky is filled with waterfowl leaving their nesting areas on their daily feeding flights.

Typically, most of the duck and goose flying occurs during the early morning hours and late afternoon hours. You might think it is boring to sit in a blind for 10 to 12 hours, but it is far from boring.

When it gets slow, you can get out and rearrange your decoys. This probably does not do any good; however, it makes you feel better—as though you are contributing to the attraction of ducks to your blind. You can always take a walk to the Banks, which only takes about 30 minutes, and if you are in the marsh, you can explore the mysteries it has to offer. Eating is always a pleasant pastime, and of course, you can always tell "war stories," bullshit, or just take a nap.

The thing that is so deceiving about this "down time," and I have never known it to fail, is that just as you think nothing is going to happen, a flock of ducks will fly by your blind not 20 yards away, and they are gone before you can get your gun up and shoot. We have learned over the years that you simply cannot relax. If you do, an opportunity will fly by you for sure.

It was not terribly cold that first day, and we were lulled into feeling pretty well secure. The guides warned us that night at dinner to bring all the clothes we had the next day because it was going to be a lulu! We wore everything we had, but we were not prepared for that kind of cold.

The second morning was somewhat slow, and James came to check on us about 10:00 am as he usually did. By then, we were quite cold but did not want to admit it to ourselves, much less to James. After all, we did not want to be thought of as tenderfoots. Charlene was already quite a novelty at Cedar Island because none of the guides had ever taken a woman duck hunting who lasted beyond 9:00 am the first day. Charlene's reputation as a bona fide, durable duck hunter was being made, and she did not want to destroy this new-found image.

Since it was slow, James suggested that we should move to another location, and we agreed. In fact, it felt good just to move around a bit and get in the boat for a ride under the "house." When James dropped us off at our next location, he said that he would return about 1:00 pm since it was so cold and make sure we were doing okay. With much "bravado," we said that we would be fine, and he bade us farewell and good hunting. It was unbelievably cold, and it was getting colder as the wind began picking up. My wind chill meter indicated that it was about 40° below zero with the wind chill, and I wished that I had not even looked at it.

It was still quiet where we were, but it was quieter than usual somehow. It took me a little while to figure out why it was so quiet—Charlene had not said anything in about an hour. It was now about noon, and I looked over to her, and she was completely doubled over holding onto her ankles. I asked her if she was all right, and all she said was that she was so cold she could not straighten up. I asked her if she wanted to go in when James came at 1:00 pm, and she said that would be fine with her. Secretly, that is exactly what I wanted too, but I did not want to admit it.

When you are that cold, it saps all your energy, and by the time we got back to the motel and took a shower, all we could do was fall into bed and sleep. We awoke in time for dinner and joined all the other hunters and guides to talk about the day. We were glad to hear them talk about it being one of the worst days they had ever experienced as far as cold went, and it did not hurt our feelings to learn that almost all of the other hunters had come in early as well.

Our first experience at Cedar Island was not a resounding success from the waterfowl kill perspective, but in every other sense, it was a wonderful time, and we vowed to do it again. However, I decided that in the future, I would make some changes, and one of those would include a heater in the blind for just such situations as our second day. I was not going to let the weather keep me from my appointed rounds with the birds.

Another tradition was begun that year, and it involved the "sinking boat." About 300 yards from the bridge where Cedar Island actually begins, there is a canal on the right side of the road where fishermen dock their boats. We noticed a boat that was docked there and partially under water. We took a picture of it out of curiosity. As it turns out, the boat was apparently abandoned and left to rot. Each succeeding year that we have gone, we always stopped to take another picture of the progress of decay. This past year, our 13th, only about 8 to 10 inches of the bow and stern remained above water. A silly tradition, I suppose, but one we have kept through all the years.

Other things I determined from that first hunt were that we would start taking some hot food or drink to the blind to help keep us warm, and that a 10 gauge shotgun was a must if you hoped to get any of the high fliers and the geese.

Finally, one other tradition that sort of evolved over the years was staying an extra night so we could return fresh and stopping at Wilbur's in Goldsboro for some more barbecue before returning home.

Also, if you have a fresh day to return, you have more time to reflect on the experience and talk about all the wonderful things that happened. If you leave after a long day in the blind, you are faced with a long drive home, you arrive exhausted, and there isn't much time to savor the experiences.

James and His Famous Biscuits

James' wife, Rachel, a true helpmate in the finest sense of the word, was gone on vacation during one of the hunts. Normally, the guides ate breakfast at the motel each morning while we were getting dressed, so at least James had some nourishment in Rachel's absence.

It seems, however, that he was on his own for dinner, and one evening, I noticed that James had an ornament hanging around his neck. Now this was in the days when men did not wear earrings or gold chains around their necks, so I knew that something was peculiar.

It was about the size of a half dollar and had a hole drilled in the middle with a string through it, which was what held it around his neck. I noticed that the guides were ribbing James unmercifully about something, and I went to see what it was about. Ira Paul asked me what I thought of James' new piece of jewelry, and I commented that it looked quite attractive on him, and they all burst out laughing. Then Ira Paul told James to show me his "biscuit," at which point James took off his ornament and handed it to me. It was hard as a rock, and they claimed that the only way James got a hole in the middle was to drill it in there with a power drill.

It seems that James, in his desperation without Rachel to cook for him, had attempted to make himself some biscuits, and this rock solid ornament was the result. His fellow guides warned him about the fish warden watching him during the day to make sure that he did not throw any of his "biscuits" and kill fish, which would, of course, have been illegal.

Newt and His Blowout

Newton Robinson is well liked by everyone but was always "bad news" when he came to hunt. Newt, as he is called by the "goides" (that is the way it is pronounced at Cedar Island), has the reputation as an accident just looking for a place to happen. In fact, he is so prone to mishaps that none of the guides want to carry him in their boat.

One time, he was in James' boat when they managed to run a fish stick through the hull of the boat, and all of the party arrived back at the dock with about a foot of water in the boat. No one was ever in any immediate danger, but, as you might expect, everyone believes it would not have happened had Newt not been in the boat.

One of the most famous stories about Newt was when he singlehandedly brought down a complete blind into the water.

The blinds at Cedar Island are nothing more than plywood boxes with eye slits in them for watching for ducks with a hard 2x10 for a seat, and each year, they are nailed onto large poles that have been drilled into the sound's bottom with air drills. If it rains during the night, it is not uncommon to find your blind with about one to two inches of water on the floor. When this happens, the guides tell you to blow a couple of holes in the bottom so the water will drain out. If you do not do this, you can spend an awfully uncomfortable day trying to keep your gear dry and out of the water.

Now most sane people will select a low, unobtrusive spot in the blind in which to create the drain hole. A side note—you must be careful when making these drain holes or you will be covered with a backsplash of water and gunpowder residue—it is best to stand up on the seat and turn your face away before pulling the trigger.

A lot of people at Cedar Island are convinced that Newt is not sane, and I guess his experience with the water drain goes a long way toward proving this theory. Instead of picking the typical unobtrusive spot, Newt proceeded to blast away at the center of the blind.

As it turned out, he managed to blow away the main 2x4 support beam under the blind, and both he and his partner went straight through the blind and into waist deep water—gear and all. Remember that this is about 6:30 am, and the guides have gone. It is cold, and these two hunters, typical of all of us, are carrying about 75 pounds of assorted gear into the blind (heaters, food, shells, shell and gear bags, guns, etc.).

It must have been rather frustrating to be standing in cold, waist deep water, holding all your gear for three or four hours and watch ducks buzz and land in your decoys and be unable to even get to your gun, much less shoot at them.

The Famous Cedar Island Buffleheads; AKA Buffalo Brains; AKA Dippers

Ducks are difficult enough to "hit" because of their speed and ability to sneak up on you when you are convinced there is nothing in the sky for at least two miles around your blind.

Buffleheads make hitting regular ducks a piece of cake. These little birds not only fly fast but have the ability to bob and weave and dart, much like doves—and besides that, completely dressed out, a large bufflehead will probably not weigh more than four ounces.

This little vignette is about an unnamed hunter I overheard talking at dinner one night about trying to kill an individual bufflehead. There are a couple of things you need to know about buffleheads in order to appreciate this story. These little birds are in abundance on the bays and sounds around Cedar Island. In fact, on slow days, you can at least count on seeing a lot of flying of buffleheads.

But they are maddening little birds. They seem to know just the precise distance to keep from your blind so they are always out of range. They will sit about 100 yards from your blind and "dip" and eat all day. You can go blind watching these little farts because every time they get up to move, and you get excited thinking they will stray your way, they buzz around and sit back down approximately six inches from where they were originally sitting.

It had been a slow day for this hunter, and when one lone bufflehead started heading right for his blind, he could not believe his luck. The little bird zeroed in at about 50 miles an hour, flying a direct, true pattern for the end of his gun barrel. Just as he got into range, the hunter let go with a salvo, and the bufflehead zipped right on by.

Exclaiming that he could not understand how he could have missed, he noticed that the bird was making a wide turn and coming straight at him again. He hurriedly reloaded and let go three more rounds as the bird bobbed and weaved and dipped right over the blind again. Incredulous that he missed again, he realized that the bufflehead was making still another pass. Fully reloaded, he waited until the bird was virtually on top of him and fired three more times, only to see the duck whiz by again. Believe it or not, here he came again, and three more shots were fired with the same results.

The hunter's rather profound conclusion about the experience was that "buffleheads do not die from noise or fright."

The Frozen Shotgun

It gets awfully cold at Cedar Island sometimes, and one morning, it was particularly cold and rainy. Since there was a lot of fog and drizzle, we just kept our guns covered with large garbage bags to keep moisture from running down the gun barrels into the actions.

The only way we could have shot anyway would have been if a bird had landed, out of desperation, in our decoys. The fog was so thick you could not see for more than 20 or 30 yards from the blind. Also, the drizzle was freezing as it fell and was making a most uncomfortable morning of it.

One of the pairs of hunters who had gone out with us that morning came by with James about 9:30. James said they were going in and wanted to know if we wanted to go also. We declined, being ever optimistic that the rain would soon halt and the birds would begin to fly.

It was later that night that we learned why these hunters elected to go in, and I really do not blame them. It seems that shortly after they had gotten into their blind, some ducks tried to land in their decoys. One of the hunters jumped up to shoot, took off the safety, pulled the trigger, and nothing happened. Figuring that his gun had jammed for some unknown reason, he set it in the corner of his blind, planning to use his spare, and forgot about it.

Since the visibility was so poor, both of these hunters decided to take a little nap and wait on the weather. The weather began to warm ever so slightly, and about 9:00, they were both startled awake with a shotgun blast going off in their blind. Upon becoming fully awake, they saw that the corner of their blind was missing, and the shotgun that was "jammed" was in the water.

What had happened was that water had trickled down the barrel into the mechanism and frozen. When the trigger was pulled, nothing happened, but when the weather warmed enough to thaw the frozen mechanism, the trigger fired. Since the gun was leaning against a corner post, it blew that off, and a nice $500 gun was lying on the bottom of the sound full of salt water.

This seemed funny at the time, particularly the way the hunters told it on themselves, but it had shaken them up enough to come in and had ruined a good day of hunting—all out of carelessness.

The Charlie Maddry 'Stomp'

Contrary to what you might think, this is not a Cedar Island dance step. Charlie has a bad knee from an old motorcycle accident when he was a patrolman in Durham, North Carolina. When we first started going to Cedar Island, Charlie tried to gamely chase down his share of ducks, but in cold weather, his leg would stiffen so badly that he could hardly climb in and out of the blind.

On this occasion, it was shortly after the authorities had taken redheads off the endangered species list, and we were allowed to hunt them. At that time, in the late 70s and early 80s, Cedar Island was a refuge for redheads. They were there literally by the thousands in individual flocks. There were times when the sky was actually "dark" with clouds of redheads as they would fly by.

We are all taught not to "flock shoot," but the temptation gets to the best of us when the sky is so full of ducks that you cannot pick out a single duck at which to shoot.

This was one of those days, and Charlie was pressed into chasing ducks simply because there were too many to run down. In one of the passes of these hoards of redheads, Charlie knocked one down, but it was only wounded. He immediately jumped out of the blind, at least as quickly as a cripple can jump, and started after the bird.

As he got close to the duck, it would dive under the water and swim a few feet. When it would dive, Charlie would let go with a shot only to get sprayed with salt water and then see the duck surface 10 or 15 yards away. On one of these shots, the bird was hit again but was still alive. As Charlie approached the bird, it dived again but this time could not swim very far. Charlie did not want to shoot it again at such close range because it would destroy the duck for eating or mounting, so he simply tried to run it down.

Now, if you have never tried to run in chest waders in knee deep water, then you have no idea how difficult that is. If you even slightly lose your balance, down you go to spend a miserable wet day in the blind. Charlie's answer was to try and step on the bird long enough to hold it in one place and be able to pick it up. Well, this bird wasn't that dead, and every time Charlie would raise his leg to try to step on the bird, it would move a few inches, playing tag with him.

It was quite a sight to see this grown man, with all this hunting gear on, dancing around in the sound like he had Mexican jumping beans in his boots. He finally got the bird, but it was not without a lot of effort and a lot of entertainment for me.

He Div!—He Div Again!

Language at Cedar Island is something you simply have to develop an ear for, and no amount of study, other than exposure to it, will help you understand what is being said. Some of the more common phrases I have already discussed, but one day while hunting with James, in his excitement, I heard a new phrase I had not heard before.

Charlie and I were hunting together, and it had been a slow day on the Outer Banks blinds. About noon, James came to tell us that it was supposed to start blowing pretty good that afternoon, and he thought we ought to move into a marsh blind.

When it blows hard near the Banks, two things happen: the guides want to go in early, and if you have ever made that 20 mile run bouncing your head off the top of the "house" on the boat in four to six foot seas, you can sympathize with their desire to "get out before she blows." The other thing that you can count on is that the ducks, sensing the coming gale winds, will head for the marsh to find a quieter place to nest for the night.

When James suggested we move, no complaints were heard from us. This was also in the days when the bluebills, Greater and Lesser Scaup, were in abundance at Cedar Island. These are strange birds to the extent that they are even dumber than redheads when it comes to their patterns of behavior. Even after being shot at, they will circle and circle the blind still trying to find a place to land—with guns blaring at them at every pass.

Bluebills like the marsh since they are more akin to mallards, which are more domesticated than pintails or even redheads. With the blowing, and knowing the propensity of bluebills to invade the marsh on such occasions, we looked forward to a busy afternoon of shooting.

We were not disappointed! As an aside, this was in the days when we thought our guides at Cedar Island really knew something about duck hunting. We hadn't wised up yet to the fact that they were just commercial fishermen trying to earn a few extra bucks in fishing's off-season. As James was leaving us in the marsh blind, I asked him from which direction the ducks would likely come and about what time to be looking for them. Without cracking a smile or giving a hint that he really had no concept of the answers, he said, "They will come from the Banks, circle the bay, and head right toward your blind—look for them about 3:30, and I'll see you about 5:00!"

Well, he guessed correctly on this day. It was about 2:00 pm when we settled into the blind, and we saw a few stragglers looking for a home from then until about 3:30. At 3:30, it was as though someone had opened the Outer Bank's gates, because here they came. True to James' prediction, they came in flocks of anywhere from 10-15 to 30-40—they came in from the east (the Outer Banks, as predicted)—they circled the bay in front us and came directly at us because the wind was from the east, and they had to try and land into the wind.

We almost melted our gun barrels from 3:30 until James came to pick us up. Since the wind was blowing at our backs, unless the ducks fell in the marsh near us, they would begin to float out into the bay in front of us. We tried to keep up with how many we had shot, but after a while, it became impossible to keep up with how many were down and in which direction they had drifted. All we knew was that we had ducks all over the bay—it looked like the Battle of the Bulge—Charlie and I were the Americans and the bluebills were the Germans.

As I said before, bluebills are not known for their intelligence, and one thing that made this such easy shooting is that as they would fly by our blind contemplating a landing, we would unload six shots, knock down anywhere from two to four ducks, and then as quickly as we could reload, here they would come again for another look. Noise certainly didn't frighten them away.

They would only retreat if they, in their unexplainable wisdom, determined that this was not a suitable landing or nesting site for them that evening.

It was getting close to 5:00 pm (time for James to pick us up), and we decided that maybe we should quit shooting since we really had no concept of how many ducks were in the bay in front of us. We knew we were over the limit, and I suppose we were beginning to feel a little guilty. About that time, James came roaring through the cut from the main channel into the bay. Charlie and I decided that it would be best for him to get into the boat with James and go search for the ducks because they were all over the bay. I would stay in the blind and pack up the gear. It was getting close to twilight as Charlie boarded the skiff for the search party. As they slowly started out into the bay to pick up the quarry, I heard a strange "whooshing" sound going by my ear. It sounded like a muffled freight train. I looked up from my packing chores and saw about 40 to 50 bluebills land right in the middle of our decoys. Over the limit or not, I could not resist the temptation and began banging away. Charlie and James were searching the edges of the marsh for our game, and I was proceeding to kill another two or three ducks every two or three minutes.

They came in droves. No sooner had I shot at some that were landing, then another bunch would try to come in and land. James and Charlie were yelling something incoherently at me, but I was oblivious to their pleas because

I was fighting my own war with "attacking bluebills" by the score.

It was a personal war—these little kamikazes were buzzing in from all directions, and I was banging away just to protect myself—you understand?

Finally, it became so dark that all I could hear was the splashing down of duck after duck as they came in to land, totally oblivious of me, James, and Charlie, and the boat, the motor, etc.

When James got back to the bank, there were at least 12 to 15 more ducks to pick up. I told him that there were a couple that were just wounded near the far edge of the marsh, and we agreed to try to find them as we headed into port.

We loaded all our gear into the boat, and James suggested that I keep one gun loaded just in case the wounded birds were lively enough to try and escape.

We located one near the edge of the marsh, and as James maneuvered the boat into position to try and pick it up, it immediately dove and swam under the boat using its wings for propulsion. This intrigued James because I doubt he had ever seen a duck swim underwater. Neither had I or Charlie for that matter! Every time the duck would surface, I tried to put a shot into it, but it seemed to sense the shot was coming, would dive again, swim 10 or 15 yards, and then resurface. It became a battle of wits between James and the duck. I sincerely think that James became oblivious to Charlie and me as he pursued his mystery duck. Finally, as the duck continued to elude him, his frustration took over. Sopping wet from trying to catch the duck bare handed, he leaned over one more time as the duck dove again, and James yelled, "He div'—he div' again!"

All we could talk about on the way in was how that stupid duck "div' and div' and div' again." A new word to me in Cedar Islandese.

Famous Last Words—"You Can Wade Here!"

At Cedar Island, the guides do not stay with you in the blinds as they do in Maryland and the Chesapeake area duck hunting preserves. I think that is one of the reasons that I prefer Cedar Island. I really do not want some hot-shot guide in my blind shooting ducks that I miss and then telling me they belong to my limit. If I am going to miss them, fine—but the ones I bring home, I want them to be mine!

Since we do not have a guide in the blind and dogs are totally useless at Cedar Island, chest waders are required for retrieving your downed ducks. In fact, if you do not have waders, you don't get any ducks.

The water over which we hunt is anywhere from a foot to three feet deep, and if you knock one down, you had better get moving, particularly if the wind is up—or he will be gone before you can catch up to him.

On this particular day, we were hunting in the same marsh blind where we were later invaded by the bluebills. It was our first experience in this blind, and it sat right on the edge of the marsh. A small bay was in front, and as we got out of the boat, Charlie asked James if we could wade here to retrieve our ducks. It is always a good idea to ask since we do not know the waters, and sometimes the guides might not remember to tell you that you can wade in one direction but not another. As James left, he said, "Sure, you can wade here without any trouble, but the bottom is soft, so go slowly."

The marsh is quite murky, and it is impossible to see the bottom if it is more than a foot deep. We could see no hint of the bottom, but trusting as we were, we took James at his word.

You must remember that Charlie has a bum knee and is not very mobile. Since this was one of our first trips to the island, I guess he was embarrassed to ask me to retrieve his ducks for him, so he was trying to do it himself—with great difficulty, I might add. He had no problem walking, but getting in and out of a blind that is eight or ten feet above the water with steps that are not designed by an architect was quite a difficult chore for him.

It wasn't long before Charlie downed his first bird, and since the wind was coming from the east (at our backs), the duck immediately began drifting away from us.

Charlie jumped from his seat and ran to the edge of the marsh. He paused for a moment, and I asked, "What's wrong?" He said, "I sure wish I could see the bottom—it looks awfully deep to me." I said, "Yeah, I know, but James said it was okay." That seemed to be all the encouragement Charlie needed as he sat down on the side of the bank and slid off into the murky waters. Before I could say "The duck is over there," Charlie bounded back up out of the water as though he had jumped onto a trampoline. I thought he had been bitten by a snake—I had never seen a man move so fast, particularly one with a bad leg. I immediately saw the problem—the water line was up to Charlie's neck.

Now, there is something you need to know about Charlie Maddry. I know of no human, with the possible exception of myself, who hates to get wet worse than Charlie. Charlie is the greatest hunter I know—the best shot I have ever seen—and he can hike your legs off hunting big game animals if you let him. But let it start raining, and it will ruin his whole day.

It was only about 7:00 am, and Charlie was already wet—his jacket was wet—water had gotten into his waders—his feet squished when he walked—and he was generally miserable. Fortunately, it was not an overly cold day, and we had a heater in the blind. To Charlie's credit, he stuck it out—but without attempting to wade any more that day.

Later, we found out the all-important fact that James "forgot" to tell us. You can wade in this little bay, but the point where Charlie attempted to get in is the point where the skiff docks to unload hunters. Because of the big engines they use, the prop had, over time, dug about a six to eight foot hole in that very spot where Charlie jumped in. Not knowing that, we declined to do any more wading that day until James returned. We let him retrieve our downed ducks.

When we knew where it was safe to wade and where it was not, we could do our own wading, and we retrieved the rest of our booty that day.

Those Pintails Had on Oxygen Masks

There are those days duck hunting when you cannot seem to hit the broad side of a barn, and then there are those days when you just can't seem to miss. This is a story about one of those better days.

Charlie and I were put into an island blind that was on the tip of a small curl of land with the sound on one side and a bay on the other. It was the only time I have ever been in that particular blind before or since. I keep trying to figure out exactly where it was so I can request it, but I have no idea exactly where it is located.

Up to this particular day, it had been slow. James had said that if it did not pick up that morning for us, he would move us to a special blind that Jerry Gaskill had given him permission to use. I think it was the personal blind of the owner of the motel, but I cannot be sure.

Charlie and I had been wanting to get some pintails, a prize duck at Cedar Island, all during this trip. About the only place you can find pintails at Cedar Island is at the Outer Banks' blinds. We had been hunting there every day, and the only ones we saw were so high it would have taken a seven-millimeter Howitzer to bring them down.

We started the day at the Banks again, but by 10:00 am, James had picked up his decoys and moved us to this marsh blind. All I know for sure is that it is north of where we usually hunt on Core Sound and due east of the motel. James said that if we had to, we could actually walk back to the motel—even though we were several miles east of it.

When we got to the blind, the water in the bay side was so shallow James had to let us off on the sound side, and we walked, with the decoys, the last 100 yards or so. At this point, we were so desperate for some good shooting that we would gladly have walked a half mile with decoys if it promised to be worth it.

Once settled, we were quite dismayed to find that just across the bay were two more hunters in another blind. Sometimes that spells real trouble at Cedar Island.

Cedar Island attracts rank amateurs as well as good shooters, and if you find yourself anywhere near the "sky-busters" (those who shoot at ducks and geese when they can barely be seen in 10-power binoculars), you are in for a long day. These people will shoot at anything that moves once it is in visible eyesight, and what happens is, because of their impatience, they tend to flare the ducks before they get anywhere near shooting range.

We soon learned that these nearby hunters were pretty good—at least they weren't "sky-busters," so we relaxed a bit.

About two o'clock, the action picked up quickly. Pintails seemed to be coming from every direction, and they all wanted to come at least close enough for us to get a shot.

Now Charlie is a great shot. Whenever he pulls down on a duck, I "expect" it to fall, and when it doesn't, I am surprised. I am not a bad shot myself, but that day, neither of us could miss. It got so ridiculous that anyone seeing us from a distance would have accused us of "sky-busting" since we were shooting at them so high. The only difference was, when we shot, down they came. We could not believe our own abilities, or "luck." All afternoon, we scored on impossible shot after impossible shot. Late in the afternoon, we noticed that the hunters across the bay from us had quit shooting and were just standing in their blind watching us as we knocked down pintail after pintail.

That evening at dinner, James asked us to come over to a certain table after we had finished our dinner—he wanted to introduce us to some people. We went, not quite knowing what to expect. The two gentlemen we met were long-time Cedar Island duck hunters, and they paid us the supreme compliment. They said that today they had witnessed some of the finest waterfowl shooting they had ever seen, and one of their parting comments stuck with Charlie and me, and we quote it even today—"Some of those pintails you guys shot were so high they were wearing oxygen masks!"

    This kind comment from two experienced hunters made us both feel good but also accomplished another purpose—it raised our guides' estimation of our abilities to a new respect, and I honestly feel it helped us gain their acceptance as "almost locals" in a very clannish little east coast North Carolina community.

Have-a-Lock, Have-a-Lock, Have-a-Lock Today!

Have you ever noticed how some things seem to irritate the heck out of you but you don't know exactly why?

In the early days of Cedar Island duck hunting trips, I took a client of mine on two or three trips. Dick Whittington and I became pretty good friends during his days at Liggett & Myers Tobacco Company. Dick was an avid duck hunter and would go at the drop of a hat. Since he was a client and loved to hunt, I invited him to go to Cedar Island.

On the way to the island, you pass through Havelock, North Carolina. I swear, after going two or three times with Whittington, if there were another route to Cedar Island other than through Havelock, I would have taken it. Every time we would pass the sign that said "Welcome to Havelock," Whittington would burst into this ridiculous song, "Have-a-Lock, Have-a-Lock, Have-a-Lock Today!" I cannot, for the life of me, remember where the tune comes from, but it was a familiar tune, and he thought this was just hilarious. I made the terrible mistake of laughing with him the first time he did it. After all, he was a client, and you always laugh at clients' jokes, don't you? The problem is that he would not shut up. He would sing this damn ditty all the way through Havelock.

Now, Havelock is not a big town, but like so many small towns, three-fourths of the town's tax dollars are invested in traffic lights so tourists will have to stop every 200 yards. I suppose the city fathers feel that if you have to stop and look around waiting for the light to turn green, maybe fatigue will finally get to you, and you will pull off and patronize one of the local merchants.

Going through Havelock with Whittington became a dreaded experience. In fact, I am convinced it is one of the reasons that I quit inviting him to go to Cedar Island—I could not find a way around that little town. And he would sing that stupid little tune at least 50 times from city limit to city limit.

Even today, I cringe when I see the welcome sign, and I haven't heard that dumb song in 10 years.

Red Drawers Flapping in the Breeze

If there is anything more dreaded than having to use the bathroom in a duck blind, I do not know what it could be. I am talking about serious bathroom going—not just relieving your bladder.

Remember now, you are in a box that is maybe four feet by six feet, with 75 pounds of gear stowed precariously all around you so that movement is already limited. The very last thing you want is a bowel attack out there. The doors on these blinds are wood with nails sticking out in odd places, and if that door is open and the wind is blowing, hanging your ass, or anything else of value, out the door for any length of time can be dangerous to your health and your sex life.

Dick had had an upset stomach the night before but insisted that he was okay to go hunting the next morning. I noticed that about 9:30 am he began fidgeting something fierce and could not seem to be able to keep his mind on watching for the ducks. The wind was pretty strong that morning—about 20 knots—and even the blind was swaying a little because of the wind.

After a while, Whittington got up and announced the dreaded words, "I've got to take a dump!" I said something like "You must be kidding—nobody does that out here." He said that if he didn't do it now, he was going to fill up the blind with it, so I could either help him or wade around in it inside the blind for the rest of the day.

There was no choice! I asked, "How do you want to handle this?" After a survey that would do an engineer proud, he pronounced that he would take off his clothes, open the door, and try to keep his feet inside the blind while hanging his butt outside the door. My job was to hold the door so it did not swing back and knock him ass over head into the blind in the middle of his emergency defecation.

When he started to strip down, I could not believe my eyes. The guy was wearing a dyed red union suit with a flap over the rear—these things had not been popular since my grandfather wore them. We started laughing so hard about it that he said that we had better shut up or it was going to go all over the blind before he could get his flap down.

This is a picture that no words can do justice to. Here is a grown man, devoid of all dignity, hanging on to the top of the blind door with his heels firmly dug into the doorstep with his ass hanging as far out as possible (remember, we were in a cross wind and the slightest miscalculation would cause us both to be inundated with a substance neither of us wanted intimate contact with).

Red flap down blowing in the wind, he let it fly. It would not have been so bad had he not had an upset stomach, but what emerged was anything but solid, and it flew everywhere. I can tell you this, I doubt if any fish live within a half mile of this event—the water was stained for the rest of the day despite the high wind. It would just not go away. It seemed to linger as a constant reminder to take the proper "stopping up" medication if you ever think there is even the remotest possibility that you may ever have to repeat Whittington's red flap experience while in a stilt blind duck hunting on a cold and windy day.

Just Keep Going—You Can Make It

This is another Dick Whittington story, but it is not funny—in fact, it was quite scary.

We had arrived early in the afternoon before the day we were to begin our hunt. After unpacking and getting settled in the room, we decided that we would walk up the beach behind the motel a little ways to see what was there. Maybe if we got lucky, some ducks would get careless and fly by.

Distance can be quite deceiving when you are unfamiliar with your surroundings. The motel sits on the banks of Pamlico Sound, and large dunes block your view of the inland part of the island when you are on the back. After walking about two or three miles up the beach at a casual pace, we decided to climb the dunes to see what was behind them. A very interesting sight greeted us as we ascended about a 20 foot sand dune.

Laid out before us was a small sawgrass field, and immediately beyond that was a beautiful little bay. Upon close examination with binoculars, Dick spotted a duck blind on the banks and a couple of flocks of ducks sitting in the bay. Even though we didn't have any decoys with us, the temptation was too great to resist. If Whittington is anything, he is an explorer, and to him, this was an adventure.

He scrambled down the dune and waded into the sawgrass. Now, if you have never tried to walk through sawgrass, it is not something for the faint of heart to attempt. Sawgrass at Cedar Island grows out of wet marshlands to a height of about five or six feet and is as thick as fleas on a cur dog in August.

The field was no more than 200 yards across, but by the time we had made it about a third of the way, I knew we were in trouble (at least I knew that I was in trouble). Whittington seemed impervious to the obstacles because he had his eye on the prize—the distant duck blind and some unsuspecting ducks.

Another problem with sawgrass is that it very adeptly hides marsh potholes that you do not dare walk through. First of all, they are muddy and you might get your boots stuck in the bottom, and, of course, you never know how deep they are going to be. All this made the 200 yards more like 600 yards by the time we had to circumvent 10 or 15 potholes of water. I was thoroughly exhausted by the time we reached the blind and could not concentrate on anything except how in the world would we ever make it back.

We stayed and hunted for a couple of hours but soon realized that we had to retrace our steps to get out of there, so we decided to leave about 2:00 pm. Every time I think of this experience, I think of the story Jack London wrote about the man who got lost in the snow and became so exhausted he just wanted to "lie down in the warm snow and take a nap" and ended up freezing to death because it was so warm and comfortable.

As we got about halfway across the field, I knew that there was no way I was going to make it back. I told Dick that I needed to rest a while. To his credit, I think he sensed how exhausted I was and knew that if I sat down, I might not get back up, and he certainly did not have the strength to carry me out of that "swamp." Every time I asked for a rest period, he cheerfully said, "Keep going, you can make it!"

Well, obviously, we did, or I wouldn't be here chronicling all of this, but if it had not been for Dick Whittington, I might not have made it. In fact, I am sure I would not have made it had I struck out on my own on that particular adventure. The only good thing about the return trip was that Dick did not sing, "Have-a-Lock, Have-a-Lock, Have-a-Lock Today" a single time. I think if he had, I would have cheerfully shot him.

To give you an idea of the memories of that experience, even today when I see a sawgrass field, I get cold chills down my back, and no amount of money would persuade me to explore uncharted sawgrass fields on the island. It was a valuable lesson, well learned.

Don't Worry—It's Only Your Waders That Are on Fire!

It didn't take us long to realize the value of heaters in the blind. In fact, they served more than one purpose.

We use 8,000 BTU Coleman catalytic heaters simply because they are so much more reliable than any others we have tried. Once we tried to save money buying some cheap fuel to use in them. Boy, did we learn a valuable lesson. Once lighted with this "inexpensive fuel," the smoke billowing out of the blind while they burned down to the heating stage was so black and intense that Charlie and I had to send our clothes to be cleaned. There was a layer of soot on our jackets thick enough to write your name on—like kids enjoy writing "wash me" on dirty cars.

Besides doing a superb job of heating the blind, these little heaters have a cap on them designed to put out the catalytic heater when you are finished using them. Once the cap is on, you can transport the heaters without fear of tipping them over and having a fire.

On top of the heater is a "grille-like cover" designed to keep your hands off the element that is burning the catalytic fuel. When you want to extinguish the heat, you raise up the grille cover and put on the cap. That immediately snuffs out the vapors that are being burned that generate the heat.

Being resourceful hunters, as we are, we quickly learned that if you put the cap "on top of the grille" with the food beneath it, it quickly became an oven. Boy, have we enjoyed some great hot lunches in the duck blind on blustery cold days because of this discovery.

Sometimes when the wind is blowing, even in an enclosed blind, the heaters can be a little difficult to light. You have to invert the heater so that the fuel drips through and makes a spot about the size of a silver dollar on the padding underneath the protective grille. Once the spot appears, you set the lighter upright and light it with a match or a cigarette lighter.

Another little tip for aspiring waterfowlers using the little heaters—bring along a full Zippo lighter for this purpose. Butane lighters do not do well in the wind, and they can burn your fingers since you have to hold them on the surface of the heater while it catches on fire. Zippos, on the other hand, can be held by the open top portion and be allowed to burn as long as necessary, with a large flame that doesn't blow out, until the heater catches and begins to burn.

Sometimes, even though the heater lights up and burns down, as it is designed to do, little heat comes out, and it is necessary to relight the heater.

On this day, it was unusually windy, and we had great difficulty getting the heater going—even huddled around it to try and keep the wind off of the flame. It finally got going, but the flame was not too high, and intuitively, I knew I was going to have to go through the relight process. I had done this many times, and I knew that if I did not get enough fluid on the padding while the heater was inverted, it would still not light as it should and we would be there all morning trying to get it going.

It was cold, and we would want some hot food soon, so a good, steaming heater was necessary. I decided to not waste any time. After all, if a silver dollar size spot is supposed to light the heater under normal circumstances, why not just hold it inverted and saturate the whole damn pad and "boom," we would have a fire in no time. Sounded like a good idea at the time.

So I held the heater inverted for much longer than necessary. There were two things I did not know at that time. First, once a heater had been lighted once, even though it did not take too well, it took very little fuel to relight it and get a roaring fire. Second, I did not realize that while I was holding it for this extended period of time, quite a lot of fuel was also dripping on the toes of my waders.

When I returned the heater to an upright position, I bent over and fired up my Zippo. The Zippo was about a foot away from the heater when the heater roared to life with a flame about three or four feet high—about three times what it is supposed to be. Not only had I done a marvelous job of "restarting" the heater, I had managed to set my waders on fire at the same time. I really did not realize this because I was too busy jumping back from the bonfire we had created and trying to get my gear out of the way of this blaze that was overtaking our blind. Charlie turned around and yelled, "You are on fire!" I immediately noticed that flames were leaping about a foot into the air from the boots of my waders. At first I tried to stomp it out, but it was gaining on me. The only solution was to get into the water quickly, or I would be spending the day in the blind with the boots burnt out of my waders.

I quickly went down the ladder and jumped into the water to put out the fire. In the meantime, I looked up to see Charlie hanging his face over the blind as smoke was billowing out of the blind like a forest fire. The smoke was visible for at least 100 feet into the air, and Charlie would probably have been in the water too except that his path to the door was blocked by our inferno. He was hanging over the edge to keep from suffocating until the fire burned itself down.

At least that day we sure had a warm heater all day and hot food all day, but not many ducks came near us until the afternoon. I guess one of their preflight scouts was out and went back to report to the flocks that half of the sound was on fire and to avoid that area until the air cleared.

The Lady Duck Hunter

Very few women come to Cedar Island to hunt. I suppose in the 13 years I have been going there, I have not seen more than two or three, and on every occasion, they come back to the motel about 9:00 in the morning—either they just do not enjoy hunting or they cannot stand the boredom or the cold or both.

Not my wife! Charlene is the greatest trooper I have ever known.

I want to tell you a short story that has nothing to do with duck hunting just to illustrate my point. Shortly after we were married, we were on vacation in Myrtle Beach and decided that we wanted to go deep sea fishing. We had been out on the large party boats that carry about 100 people, but we had never been out on a small charter boat. We thought that it would be great fun not having to battle all the "amateurs" and catch us some really big fish.

We chartered a small boat (probably no longer than about 28 feet) and set sail for the open seas about 6:00 am one morning with about 15 people on board. About halfway out to the Gulf Stream, we went through one of the most violent squalls I have ever experienced. This storm tossed this boat not only up and down but side to side at the same time. Everybody on the boat was sick and lying down in any spot they could find.

After about an hour, we broke through the squall and the Captain announced that we were "Over the fish—everybody up and fish." Nobody moved! We were all green. I have never been so sick in my life, and I vowed that I would pay a helicopter pilot no less than $5,000 if the Captain would call one and have him pick me up and take me back to shore.

I could not move, and as I looked around me, I noticed that everybody else was lying down and looked about the same as I did—with one exception—I could not find Charlene.

The first thought that went through my mind was I wondered if she was overboard. It was a rough storm, and when I got sick, I lost all sense of where I was and what was happening. All I wanted to do was lie down, close my eyes, and pray for land. As badly as I felt, I determined it was my duty to find my wife and at least know that she was still on board somewhere.

I looked in all the normal places sick people, on the verge of death, would be, but I could not find her. Finally, I ventured out on deck, and there she was, hauling in one fish after the other.

Holding on to the railing and valiantly placing one foot in front of the other, I struggled to her position and calmly asked her what in the hell did she think she was doing. Her reply was, "I paid $30 to fish, and I am going to fish!"

She was the only one in the fishing party who was on their feet, and every time she would catch a fish, she would lean over the rail and upchuck—then bait her hook again and catch another fish. As I went back to lie down, I could not help but think how proud of her I was and what a trooper she was.

So when she readily agreed to go duck hunting with me the first time, even though she had never been duck hunting in her life and had never fired a shotgun, I knew she would do just fine.

That first night on entering the restaurant, the waitress asked us if we were guests of the motel, and I said, "No, we are hunting tomorrow." The look on her face as she looked first at me, then at Charlene, and then back to Charlene again said it all.

You see, Charlene is only five feet one inches tall and weighs about 100 pounds. She looks just like the English teacher that she is, and she certainly does not fit the macho image of the duck hunters sitting around having dinner.

The real shocker came the next morning when we came into breakfast at 5:00 am and watched all the men do double takes at this "little lady" who was dressed for duck hunting and eating with all these hairy legged men. I could just hear them under their breath saying, "I'll bet she won't last until nine o'clock." After all, that is all the others had been able to do.

Well, not only did she last, she lasted through some of the coldest weather Cedar Island had ever seen and earned the respect of every man there.

I have since overheard the guides tell other hunters, when they questioned whether Charlene was going to hunt or not, that "That little lady is a real 'duck hunter' and she can stick it out with the best of you."

No one looks at her "funny" now because not only can she "last with the best of them, she can shoot better than many of them." I am proud of my "lady duck hunter" and would take her anywhere!

Does It Ever Get Cold at Cedar Island?

"Man, whatchu mean?"

I don't remember the exact year, but it was around 1981 or 1982. I used to believe that salt water could not freeze. I don't know where I got that idea, but I had always believed it.

One morning, we woke up, and at breakfast, the guides told us not to come to the dock until about 7:30 am because they had already been down there, and it was so cold that the motors would not start, and they needed time to get about two inches of ice off the boats. And, they needed to get the boats started so they could rock the harbor to break up the ice that had formed overnight.

I smelled a rat. I thought maybe the guides just didn't want to go blasting across the sound at about 30 knots per hour in sub-zero temperatures and they were just buying a little time until the sun came up.

When we got to the harbor, I realized that it was worse than I had imagined. All the boats were running now and rocking in the water. The ice was solid for about 200 yards out past the entrance to the harbor.

James had scraped enough ice off his boat that we could safely board, and he told us to get on board and we would try to get out of the harbor. Apparently, the water was clear out past the 200 yard frozen area. He explained that we would have to back out and try to break up the ice with the rear of the boat. He explained that the wooden boats could not confront the ice head-on or it might cut into the wooden hull. This turned out to be a long and arduous project.

First, he would have to throw out a heavy anchor as far as he could in front of the boat to attempt to break the ice. Then, in reverse, he would gun the engine and ram the ice from the rear, breaking a small patch at a time. About 10:00 am, we finally cleared the ice and began our run to the Outer Banks, but another surprise awaited us.

The wind had howled all night, making the wind chill factor about 40° below zero. By the time we got to the first blind, the wind had blown the waves continuously up over the steps to the blind, and at least a solid foot of ice was wrapped around each step leading up to the blind. It was not possible to ram the blind with the boat in hopes of breaking the ice because the wooden steps were so brittle they would easily break. The only option was to use a carpenter's hammer James had on the boat to chip away at the ice on each step enough to get a foothold and climb into the blind.

As you might imagine, this took about an hour at each blind, each person taking his turn standing in freezing cold water, chipping away, and in the process freezing his hands and getting his gloves soaking wet.

Finally, about noon, we were all placed in our blind. In ours, the first order of business was to fire up the heater—the hell with the ducks and what they might see—we were freezing. In short order, we warmed up and had a good day of hunting for the rest of the day.

Does it get cold at Cedar Island? You bet your Coleman heater it does! Can salt water freeze—I've got the pictures to prove it!

Can One Be Comfortable With His Waders Filled With Water?

Absolutely not! But it can happen.

This was another one of those bitterly cold days when Dick Whittington and I were hunting. In fact, it was so cold and frozen over on this particular day that even the guides could not get out in the boats, even by backing out past the ice. The ice would just not budge.

Dallas Goodwin and Clyde Styron had an idea. They told Dick and me to get our stuff together, and they would take us up the beach to a place where they thought we might get some shooting.

I noticed as we piled into their truck that they also loaded two or three wood axes into the back along with some decoys. At the time, I could not imagine what they intended to do with the axes.

They told us to pack light because the last few hundred yards would be on foot because they could not take the truck all the way to the place they had in mind. We drove about five or six miles up the beach and then turned into a little cove where the road abruptly stopped at a sawgrass field. Now, you know how I feel about sawgrass, but fortunately, there was a small path in the direction we were going.

Dallas and Clyde both loaded bags of decoys on their backs, picked up their axes, and beckoned us to follow with our guns, lunches, and ammo. We hiked for what seemed like half the day and finally came to a peninsula that jutted out into a bay that I did not even know was there. It was a beautiful day, but the bay was frozen solid. Dallas told us to get into a make-shift blind that was nearby, and he and Clyde began chopping about a 20x30 foot hole in the ice to put our decoys into.

I knew no ducks would come by with all that activity, so I asked Dallas if I could wade around in this area. He said, "Sure, but be careful about the ice because it would cut the waders like a hot knife would cut butter."

For some reason, the water right next to the marsh was not frozen, I suppose because what waves there were kept pounding the shoreline. It was frozen about four or five feet out into the bay, but not right up against the marsh. So, to pass the time, I started wading around the edge of the inlet just to see what it felt like.

The bottom there was soft but navigable. I had gotten about 75 or 100 yards away from the ice chopping activity when I noticed that the water was gradually getting deeper. I did not think much about it because Dallas had said I could wade here, and Dallas was a guide and knew all about these things.

With the next step, I went into a hole that came at least four or five inches above the tops of my waders. I was too far from the bank to grab some reeds, and I was bouncing on my tip toes hoping that the water would not get any deeper. Each time I bounced up, I would scream "Help!" as loud as I could. I could not go backward because I could not get a foothold—I could not go forward because for all I knew, the water was even deeper. The prettiest sight I saw that morning was Clyde's hand reaching down to pull me up. He said, "What in the world are you doing all the way up here?" I replied that Dallas said I could wade here, and Clyde just laughed—"He didn't mean up here halfway back to the motel—he meant down there where we are chopping ice for the decoys."

Clyde then asked me if I had gotten wet. This was in the days when I was still a novice duck hunter and certainly did not want to tarnish my own macho image, so I naturally said, "No, I'm fine!" There must have been six inches of water in my boots, and it was getting colder by the moment. I stupidly toughed it out until they left and then came out of my waders, emptied the water, and Whittington saved the day by lending me a pair of his dry socks. My feet were still colder than I would have liked, but I survived.

The main lesson I learned is that "machoness" is not what it is cracked up to be. Better a warm wimp than a frozen macho man! If that happened today, I would beat a hasty retreat to the motel, shower, redress, and be a lot more comfortable than the miserable time I spent in that out of the way blind that day just because my pride got in the way.

Down Here, We Call That a "SHELLDRAKE"

While Cedar Island offers some of the finest waterfowl shooting to be found on the east coast, it does have its share of "bluebird" days. Bluebird days are those days when, for whatever reason—usually beautiful weather—nothing flies. I mean, it is even difficult to find a sea gull wandering around.

Charlene and I were hunting on this particular bluebird day. Sometimes it is difficult to occupy your time in a blind on this type of day. It was about 60 or 65°, the water was as calm as glass, and there was absolutely no wind.

Even though it is difficult to kill time on days like this, there are things you can do. If you don't create some activity, believe it or not, you will be more exhausted when you come in than had you been shooting and chasing ducks all day.

About 10:30 am, after eating the first Wrangler of the day, we decided to hike to the Outer Banks. A word of explanation to the novice—if you have never had a Wrangler, you simply have not lived. They are semi-spicy hot dogs by Hormel, and in a duck blind on a cold day, there is simply nothing to compare with a hot, juicy Wrangler lathered with mustard on a warm bun.

Since the water is pretty shallow, you can hike it from the nearer blinds in about 20 or 25 minutes. Once there, you can explore the barrier islands, look for sea shells, and, on occasion, we have been known to flush some pothole sitting ducks and bring one or two back to the blind.

So we loaded a few shells in our waders, got our guns, and headed out at a leisurely pace for the Banks. The sky was crystal clear, and the walk was actually quite pleasant. Still, no ducks flying.

We picked up a few sea shells and laid them aside for the return trip and continued on inland on the island to search for potholes. We found quite a few, but no ducks. Finally, we just sat on the edge of the marsh and looked out over the sound for about an hour. We knew that James would be coming to check on us soon, so we started back about 1:00 pm.

When he came, he suggested moving although he didn't have very encouraging news. No one was shooting anything. We moved to another blind and settled in.

After taking a short snooze, Charlene punched me and said that a duck had landed about 100 yards off the front of the blind. I looked up and saw it was much too far to shoot at. Watching it for about 30 minutes, the absence of shooting activity got to me, and I decided to take a shot.

Sometimes, when you shoot at sitting ducks from that distance, they get confused about where the shot came from and occasionally will actually fly closer to you instead of heading in the opposite direction.

Much to my surprise, the duck went "belly-up" with the impossible shot, and we had us a duck and were not "skunked" for the day. I retrieved it, and it was a strange-looking bird. It looked almost like a cross between a sea gull and a duck, but it was nothing like I had ever seen before.

We stowed it in the blind and waited out the rest of the day until James came for the trip home. I showed it to James, and he looked quite puzzled. He didn't comment at first, and I have learned over time that when these guides don't immediately comment, they really have no idea what the answer is, and they are just stalling for time. When we got back to the dock, James took the bird to some of the other guides, and they huddled in conversation. When he came back, he said with as much authority as he could muster, "Down here, we call that a shelldrake."

Freely translated, that meant he still had no concept of what it was, but being a guide, he couldn't simply admit that—instead, he had invented a duck that I would challenge anyone to find in any waterfowl book published in the free world.

Oh well, at least we had us "something," and most of the groups had nothing to show for their day. In fact, we had us a "Shelldrake"—whatever that is!

It's Another World—And Another Language

If you have read many of these stories, you probably know by now how much I am in love with Cedar Island. It is truly another world. It is only accessible by one road, or the ferry from Ocracoke. The people who live there live very special, hard-working lives. There is only one grocery store, one gas station, one post office, one Methodist church, one major boat dock, and about 250 hearty souls who work from before sunup to after sundown.

In fact, if you need car repairs or tires, have to go to school, need to buy clothes, need a doctor or a hospital, the nearest facilities are in either Beaufort or Morehead City—about 35 miles away.

If you were to wander onto Cedar Island by mistake, you would probably think you were in a foreign country because of the language. It is sort of a cross between Chesapeake waterman slang and Cedar Island east coastese. It is difficult to decipher, and it just takes practice. Jerry Gaskill is probably the worst. When he gets excited telling a story, he talks faster than any human being alive. Couple that with twangs and unusual words, and you have to listen with all of your concentration just to try and pick up about every third word.

To give you a small taste of what it is like, one day, James came roaring up to the blind and said, "Shore is cam, ain't it!" I replied that I could not hear what he said and asked him to repeat it. He said, "It shore is slick cam—no wind at all." I figured out that "cam" must mean calm, and he must be referring to the absence of waves.

On another occasion, he said that he would be picking us up about 3:30 instead of the usual 5:00 because the "foge" (rhymes with "rogue") was going to get bad. Neither Charlie nor I knew what the "foge" was, but we conjured up all kinds of demonic pictures until we realized that James meant the fog was going to get thick and we might have trouble finding the dock.

A guide is a "goid" and a blind is a "bleund," and if you are going to attach something to yourself or your boat, you are going to "do something onto it." Of course, you already know that dive is "div" and oysters are "arsters."

Don't worry—if you ever have the chance to go and become friends with these people, it will be one of the richest experiences of your life, and you will absorb the language—it just takes a little time, but it is worth it.

John and His First Goose

I started taking my son to Cedar Island when he was about 16 years of age. They say there is such a thing as beginner's luck, but I never really believed it until I had been hunting with John.

John is a pretty good shot—we had done some squirrel hunting and had been to Nantahala hunting bear and boar before, so he had had a lot of practice. However, I knew that nothing prepares you adequately for 60 mile per hour ducks, and that increases to about 80 miles per hour in a downwind. I guess that John did not know how difficult it was.

Shortly after being in our first blind about 30 minutes, two bluebills flew in and he dropped both of them with one shot. I could not believe my eyes, yet he seemed to be nonplussed by his feat.

I had been coming to Cedar Island about six years before I got my first goose, but on our next trip, it was to be John's turn (his second trip, no less). We were in a blind near the Banks when a flock of about 12 Canada geese flew in and sat about 150 yards out off our blind.

John and I stayed down low in the blind and just watched them through the peep holes for about an hour. They swam around and fed and seemed in no hurry to go anywhere. We were really getting cramped, and John kept asking if he could take a shot. I told him that it was hopeless from this distance, and we would just have to be patient.

After about another hour, they got up and started to move. They flew to the side of our blind, still out of range, but then made an abrupt turn north right behind our blind. It was apparent they were not going to land again, nor come any closer, so I told John it was now or never, even though they were still about 70 yards out—much too far. But we wanted a goose so badly, John and I fired at the same time, and "glory be"—two geese hit the water.

John just about wet his pants, but they were only wounded—it was not a clean kill.

I yelled at him to get into the water and chase them down. I gave him some shells and told him to shoot when he got within about 30 yards. I told him to hurry because a wounded goose can outswim a walking man in waders very quickly, and if he didn't get to them soon, they would be out of reach.

John almost fell into the sound trying to get out of the blind, he was so excited. I handed him his gun when he was in the water, and then I witnessed a real case of buck fever.

John made good time and gained on the geese. He got to within about 30 yards and looked back at me as if to say, "Should I shoot now?" I signalled to go ahead, and because of his excitement, his first shot hit the water about five feet in front of him. His second shot was not much better, and it became obvious that he was so hyped up that he was going to run out of shells before he ever hit those geese with a killing shot.

I jumped out of the blind, and together, we finished them off. I have never seen a happier kid as he carried these two huge geese back to the blind by himself. I was quite content to trail along behind him and let him enjoy his glory.

John has moved several times in the past few years, but every time I have been in his house, that goose is proudly displayed in his living room, no matter where he is living. A great experience for a father and son to share.

Watch Out for the Sand Sharks When Retrieving Your Ducks!

Charlie and I were embarking on another day of hunting with James, and we were waiting at the dock for the rest of the group to arrive. We were all getting a little impatient because it was after six o'clock, and all the other guide boats and hunters had gone. No one was specifically saying anything yet, but it was obvious that James was getting a little agitated.

We asked him who was coming, and he said some new fellows who didn't get in until about one in the morning and then stayed up all night playing cards and drinking. Now, Jerry Gaskill has a very firm rule about drinking in the restaurant. You cannot even bring your own bottle in there, and he does not serve any kind of alcoholic beverages, even though I know that he could make a lot of money by just serving beer. Maybe it is just the mores or religious history of the island.

I have been privileged by being such a frequent guest and getting to know the guides pretty well that I have heard stories about the people there that would be inappropriate to tell, even in a journal such as this. Besides that, I would not violate their confidences by repeating some of the things that I have heard. The point is that I have never, not once, heard a story about anyone having a drinking problem on the island. I guess it is the old morals that have carried over from the early days and the hard work that it takes to make a go of it on Cedar Island. Drinking just does not fit in with the culture.

By and by, these two "dudes" showed up at the boat as though it was our duty to wait on them "until they were good and ready to go hunting"—even though the written and unwritten rules are, "Be at the boat dock no later than 6:00 am sharp!"

They were quite a sight. Disheveled, red-eyed, and unsteady, to say the least. I am sure a night without sleep and missing breakfast had a lot to do with it, but we all vowed not to light a cigarette on the way to the blind for fear that the alcohol fumes emanating from these two might blow us all to kingdom come before we ever left the harbor.

James is a patient man. He would have to be to work like he does, raise two boys under less than ideal conditions, and then have to put up with the likes of these two early in the morning, knowing that he would have to cater to them for the rest of the day. But James has his limits.

He didn't say much on the way to the blind, and he is usually full of chatter early in the morning. I stood up by him as we headed out, and I asked him what he intended to do with these two drunks. He said, possibly in jest, that "Maybe they would end up shooting each other and we wouldn't have to bring them back that night."

When rankled, Cedar Island guides can be cantankerous. They will do little things that only a seasoned hunter at the island would recognize.

James did it all this morning. First, he put them out as the first group of the day, just to get rid of them. All of the good shooting the previous few days had been on the Banks, and James dumped these deadbeats into the first marsh blind he came to before even clearing the sound to head for the Outer Banks blinds. Second, he only put out about 10 decoys when the normal spread for two hunters is about 35 to 50 decoys. And finally, he put them in a blind with little protection from the wind with only scrub bushes around a couple of old fish boxes to sit on. Now, I have hunted out of these types of blinds, and on a good day, when the ducks are flying, you forget about the amenities and don't think twice about it. Besides, I know that if James or Dallas puts me in one of these blinds, it is for a good reason—like a lot of expected activity and not because I offended them.

As they climbed into their blind, we could see a bottle of vodka sticking out of one of the hunter's pockets, and James just shook his head, wished them well, and told them he would be back to check on them later.

Charlie had the best and last laugh of the day. As we chugged away from their blind, Charlie called out to one of them to "Be careful of the sand sharks" when they waded to pick up any ducks they might shoot! We all had a good laugh as we headed out to our blinds.

Not until that night when James came to sit at dinner with us for a short visit did we know that these two dumbasses believed what Charlie had told them. They did not venture into the water all day long for fear of being eaten by a sand shark. By the way, there has never been a shark sighted within 300 miles of Cedar Island, but these two miscreants did not know that. Sort of served them right, don't you think? At least all of us had a good laugh over that, and the guides thought it was great!

If You Don't Sit Down and Shut Up, I'll Leave You Here All Night!

About the only thing that I have ever seen James get really riled up about is drinking among duck hunters—particularly those messing around with loaded guns in the duck blink. That really rattles his tree.

On this occasion, Charlene and I were hunting with James, and we took two more drunks out to an out of the way blind and got them out of the boat early. James was really upset and threatened not to even go back to check on them all day because he was afraid he might get shot accidentally.

From the time these two boarded the boat in the morning until they were put out into their blind, they continually complained about the decline in shooting activity at Cedar Island over the years and kept telling James to put them in the best blind on the sound—as though none of the rest of us in the boat wanted to do any shooting. In fact, I believe they thought they were the only two hunters in the boat, and there were four others of us who hoped for a good day as well.

Well, James put them out first as he usually does with people he doesn't want to be around any longer than necessary. Then he turned to the rest of us and apologized, and with a wry smile said, "I doubt it will even be necessary for them to load their guns in that blind—hasn't been a duck there in five years."

Whatever James is, he is responsible. He did go check on them that day and reported to us when he saw us that they "Still hadn't fired a shot and were mad as hell." We had a good day; both Charlene and I got our limits.

One thing you can always count on with James is that if he likes you, he will pick you up last at the end of the day, even though it might make a little extra work for him, because he wants you to have every opportunity to get your limit, or that special duck or goose you are hoping for.

On this day, James was a little late picking us up. When the guide is late picking you up, I don't know about others, but I get a little antsy. Just the thought of spending the night in one of those blinds is a little spooky. It has never happened because the guides continually check on each other, and if one has motor trouble, another will come pick you up.

But this day, it was already almost dark when James' boat came into sight. When he arrived at the blind, I noticed that only two hunters were in the boat, and I assumed he had taken the obnoxious group in early because they were not happy with their hunt. As it turned out, he hadn't even picked them up yet, but he had a reason.

When I asked him about the two malcontents, he said with a chuckle, "Let's just let them stew a little while and think that I am lost."

As you might imagine, when we finally arrived at their blind, it was well after dark, and as we approached, we could see flashlights waving back and forth trying to signal any passing boat. James simply grinned as he pulled up and casually asked them how their day had been. Mad? Whoowee, these guys were mad! They immediately started demanding why James was so late, why he had put them into a blind where there were no ducks, why he didn't come and move them to a better blind, why he didn't check on them more often, and on and on. James listened without saying a word as he stowed their gear, and we all moved around to make room for them in the boat.

When they had finished their tirade, instead of putting the engine in gear and heading for port, James reached over and shut off the engine. He then leaned down under the "house" and pointed to the two troublemakers and said, "If you guys don't just sit down and shut up, I am personally going to take you off this boat and put you on this island, and you can just spend the night here until you cool off!"

I have never heard James say anything like that before or since that incident, but it worked. They were docile and quiet all the way in, and we did not see them the next day. I guess they went home, probably never to return. However, if they ever did want to come back, I suspect they would have had great difficulty finding a guide who would take them out—in fact, they might even find that Jerry was mysteriously "booked up" on the specific days they wanted to hunt.

That SOB Just Left Me a Rusty Shotgun

As long as we are on the subject of anger, I might as well tell you the one time when I saw Jerry Gaskill angry—it only happened once because he is such a fine person and so even-tempered.

A hunter had come to hunt with the group one year and found that upon arriving, something was wrong with his shotgun. The nearest place to have any kind of gun work done is in Morehead City or Havelock, and that is an hour's drive away.

Jerry had just been given a brand new Remington 1100 for Christmas, and he willingly offered it to the hunter. In fact, I am not sure the gun had ever been fired.

The day we hunted, it rained off and on all day—although the shooting was good. Now, anyone who knows anything about guns knows that you protect your gun the best you can under inclement conditions. When it begins to rain on us, we pull out some extra big plastic garbage bags and cover our gear, and we always save one to slip over the barrel and stock of the gun to protect it from water going down the barrel and fouling up the mechanism. It is easy enough to slip that bag off when you see ducks coming, but to not protect it is asking for future trouble.

Also, when you come in that night, the first thing to do is break the guns down and clean them thoroughly with WD40 or Breakfree, just to be sure they will perform the next day.

When this hunter came in that night, he handed Jerry back his gun in the case, thanked him for the loan, and went off to dinner. Since the man was only hunting one day, he did not have the occasion to borrow it the next day. Jerry stays pretty busy running Driftwood Enterprises (two groceries, a gas station, a laundromat, the motel and restaurant, and maybe other things I do not know about), so he has little time to hunt himself. He just put the gun away in his motel office closet and forgot about it.

We were back down for another hunt about three weeks later, and after dinner one night, he called me into his office telling me he wanted to show me something. He pulled out this brand new Remington, and at first I thought it was some kind of antique or something that had washed up on the shoreline. He said, "This is my brand new Christmas present, and it is only four weeks old." It was covered with rust—the action was frozen closed and would not operate. I exclaimed, "What in the world happened to that?" He said, "Do you remember that guy that was down here when I loaned him a gun to hunt with?" I commented that I did. "Do you remember how it rained that day?" Then it came clear to me. I said, "Do you mean that he did not even try to clean the gun when he returned it?" Jerry said that he did not personally check it, which he admitted he should have, but he assumed, like I probably would have, that it would have been cleaned and dried off before being returned. "I just put it away and just took it out last weekend to do a little afternoon hunting, and this is what I found."

"That SOB gave me back a rusty shotgun!" As my mother was always so fond of saying as a way of explaining some people's behavior, "There is just no accounting for taste!" I might add "responsibility" to that phrase, and now I know what she was referring to all those years when she used that phrase.

A Most Unexpected Gift

My daughter, Lora, is 14 now, and this was to be her first year to go duck hunting at Cedar Island. I know that young girls have lots of better things to do, but her mother and I have "talked up" Cedar Island so much that I really believe she was looking forward to going.

I had called Jerry earlier with the following proposition. We planned to hunt for two days, and I asked Jerry if Lora could spend the second day with Jerry's wife, Charran, just in case Lora did not care for 12-hour stints in a duck blind. Charran called Charlene to tell her that she would be delighted to have Lora spend a day with her if duck hunting was not Lora's forte.

I also told Jerry that I was having difficulty finding "women's waders" to fit Lora, and he said, "Don't buy any until you know if she is going to enjoy it—I've got a men's size seven she can wear and just put on about three pairs of socks to fill out the shoes." So that problem, and the potential problem of not liking duck hunting, was solved. We seemed ready to go.

Our plans called for us to leave Winston-Salem the day after Christmas, spend a day at our beach house in Southport, and then drive to Cedar Island. I noticed that Charlene did not seem to be as "well" as she should be and did not seem to be showing the usual amount of enthusiasm about going. On the morning we were to leave, I found out why.

Both Charlene and Lora had come down with the flu and were quite ill. They got dressed, Lora carrying around a sauce pan in case she needed to throw up.

There is no worse feeling in the world than to be sick in a duck blind, or to even go out hunting if you are feeling the slightest bit queasy. There is no place to go once you are there, and you can be awfully miserable. I shut Lora and Charlene up in the den and said, "Both of you are adults—you talk about this and then tell me if we are going or if you both are going back to bed." Common sense prevailed, and they both went back to bed.

I called Jerry to give him the bad news, and he was several times disappointed. Jerry and Charran have been married four years now, and every year, Charlene and I have celebrated their anniversary with them on the 14th of December.

This year, because of Charlene's new teaching position at Salem Academy, she was unable to go on opening day, so we missed the anniversary celebration. Therefore, we planned to "celebrate" it again when we came down after Christmas. Charran and Jerry were disappointed because they planned to roll out the red carpet for Lora and were looking forward to meeting her. We were all disappointed because this would be the first year Charlene missed going in 13 years.

But possibly the most disappointed person of all was David, Jerry and Charran's son. David is almost 14 and had just gotten his boat and wanted to take Lora around and show her the sights in his new boat. Well, suffice it to say, we were all disappointed, but this disappointment was somewhat abated by Jerry's surprising generosity.

When I told him all of this, he said that he had "bought Lora a new pair of waders just for her and would I like for him to send them on to her?" That is the type of person he is, and we were all touched. When the waders arrived, his note said that "Lora owed him a trip to Cedar Island, and he was expecting her next year."

I believe that will be a debt Lora will enjoy repaying.

Even Ira Paul Can Get Flustered and Speechless Occasionally

Ira Paul Day was one of the "original" four guides who helped Jerry Gaskill build Cedar Island into the premier waterfowl hunting area it is today. Like the other guides, Ira Paul is a waterman by trade, but guided during the off season to pick up some extra money when fishing wasn't paying too well.

Ira is always full of stories and holds court nightly, either at the restaurant or next door at the grocery store, whether he is guiding or not. I have seen Ira a bit flustered only once in all the years I have been going to Cedar Island.

One night after dinner, we were all sitting around in the lower portion of the restaurant. The guides were swapping stories, and the rest of us were just listening and enjoying it. For the past few years, it seems that every time I came to Cedar Island, I always managed to get my limit—a large part of that I attribute to Charlie's excellent shooting ability.

I guess Ira had heard that even when other parties did not do well, Charlie, or Charlene and I, always seemed to come in with our limits (or sometimes a few above). In any case, we never seemed to get "skunked."

There was a lull in the conversation, and Ira looked over to me and said something like, "Horace, you always seem to be lucky down here, even when nobody else is doing well." Without thinking about it, I retorted, "It's skill, Ira, not luck!"—and I managed to say it with a straight face. It is times like these when I wish I had had my camera with me because the look of astonishment and incredulity that came across Ira's face was priceless, and for the first time since I had known him, he was speechless.

Then, as though it were some kind of concession and acknowledgement of my sense of humor, or sense of timing, or something, a big grin started creeping across his face. It was not a sneer, but a genuine grin of affection, and Ira and I have been fast friends ever since. It is always nice to top the king at his game, even if it only happens once in your lifetime.

Horace after a good day of hunting

Horace in a duck blind

Charlene, AKA "Fetch"

Horace and Charlie Maddry

Duck blind at Cedar Island

Driftwood Motel

Edward and Gerald Wain Gaskill, Jr.

Tragedy strikes everywhere at one time or another, and Cedar Island is no exception. Despite the fun and games we have, genuine sorrow can invade any atmosphere, and for a little while, it makes you realize how valuable your friends are, and how precious life itself really is.

Edward (Ed) Gaskill is Jerry's older brother by just a few years. I am not sure about Ed's past, but I think he was retired from some kind of government service or possibly the military when he came back to Cedar Island to live about three or four years ago.

Jerry needed help in managing the motel and restaurant, and when Ed returned, he assumed some of Jerry's responsibilities, particularly helping get us hunters off every morning, and relieved Jerry from having to get up at 3:00 am six days a week during the hunting season.

That is how I came to know Ed. Our acquaintance was rather casual until one year I was taking John to hunt. John, at this time, was starting a new job and only had one day off that he could hunt. He had to work until 6:00 pm the night before. So that put us arriving at Cedar Island at about 11:00 pm, long after the restaurant had closed and everyone else was fast asleep. What John and I did not really realize was that we were going down on New Year's evening, and there were no restaurants open as we made our way to Cedar Island.

Needless to say, by the time we arrived, we were literally starving and desperately in need of something to eat. We woke Ed up, and he graciously let us in. I asked him if there was anything left over from dinner that we could nibble on, and he searched the kitchen in vain. Then he said, "Tell you what, you go get settled in your room, give me a few minutes to get dressed, and meet me at the store next door."

We did, and Ed helped us pick out lunch meat, canned pork and beans, and cookies, and he suggested that we take a little of this and a little of that. We tried to pay him, but he refused, saying it was on the house, to enjoy, and he would see us at breakfast.

After that, I always had sort of a special place in my heart for Ed, and we always visited when I came back to Cedar Island. I always looked forward to seeing Ed. I was deeply saddened to learn that in early 1988, Ed had been diagnosed as having cancer and was not expected to live for more than a year.

Ed died around Christmas in 1988, and I happened to be hunting at Cedar Island when the funeral was held. I stayed in that day because I wanted to attend Ed's funeral. Even though I was not dressed for it, our guide at that time, Dallas Goodwin, picked me up at the motel, and I rode with Dallas and his wife Debbie to the church and then to the funeral.

It was one of the most impressive funerals I had ever attended. I had never seen a Masonic funeral before, and when I entered the church, I noticed that all the ushers wore small white aprons over their suits. It turned out they were the pallbearers.

I still don't know the significance of the aprons; however, each Mason at the funeral wore one and participated in the ceremony. The most impressive part of the funeral was at the gravesite where all the Masons stood in military fashion and chanted their own symbolic farewell to Ed Gaskill. It was all done from memory, and was most impressive.

I remember the minister, in his remarks at the church as he talked about Ed's life and virtues, kept saying that he wished he had known Edward Gaskill better during his life.

The last memory I have of Ed is really a sad one for me. As I said, we were hunting down there at the time he was so sick and due to go back to the hospital for the last time. I had asked Jerry how Ed was doing, and he said that Ed was in very bad shape, yet he still tried to get up every morning and come to the motel to help out.

One morning as I was leaving breakfast, my mind on getting back to the room and getting dressed so as not to be late, a truck pulled up out front, and a very large man got out with great difficulty. As I passed him, he cheerfully said, "Hello, Horace, how are you doing?" I replied, as so many of us do to that type of greeting, without thinking, "Fine, how're you doing?" The man replied that he was "doing pretty good."

I realized later that it was Ed Gaskill, and it was the last time I would ever see him alive—and I did not recognize him. His illness had taken such a severe hold over him that even his facial features had changed. It still haunts me today that I did not recognize Ed, and I hope that he was not offended by that.

I keep thinking now, "I wish I had known Edward Gaskill better during his life."

More bad news on the same trip. One evening on the way back to port from hunting, I was standing with Dallas in the boat as we roared across the bays and sounds. He leaned over toward me and asked me if I had heard about Wain's problem.

Wain was Jerry's oldest son and was a student at the University of North Carolina at Chapel Hill. I had been preoccupied thinking about Ed and was unaware that Wain had any problems.

I never really knew Wain, not even as well as I knew Ed. Wain used to help out at the motel and restaurant when he was home from school on break, but he was not a hunter and never went out with us, so I never had the chance to really talk to him except to speak and say hello.

Dallas told me that Wain had just been diagnosed as having AIDS. If you know the people on Cedar Island and the lifestyle they live, you would know what a foreign disease this must have been to them. It never occurred to me that Wain was gay—it is just something that was never discussed—nor, to my knowledge, had it ever happened on Cedar Island.

Well, Wain was gay and had contracted this dread disease. He was not expected to live out the year.

That night before dinner, Jerry asked me if I could stick around for a little while after dinner—that there was something he wanted to tell me. I said of course that I would, and I suspected that he wanted to tell me about Wain, not knowing that Dallas had already told me. Now, I am glad that Dallas did tell me, because I do not know how I would have reacted hearing it cold from his father.

When Jerry sat down and tried to tell me about it, he couldn't get past the first few words because tears filled his eyes and he choked up so much he could barely speak. I told him that I knew and how sorry I was. He said that they would just have to do all they could for Wain while he was alive, and just hope that the people on the island and Wain's friends would understand and be sympathetic.

Clay Gaskill is Jerry's younger son by his first marriage and Wain's blood brother. Clay is as raw-boned and tough as any fisherman on the island. Jerry had asked Clay how he felt about his brother's illness, and Clay said that he would beat anybody to shreds who said anything unkind about Wain.

During Wain's illness, he stayed at the N.C. Memorial Hospital in Chapel Hill, and Jerry and Charran spent virtually 24 hours a day at his bedside during his last few weeks. Jerry told me that one time, Wain looked up at him and said, "Daddy, I am sorry this is taking so long and is so expensive."

Probably the most impressive sight I have ever witnessed was the funeral for Gerald Wain Gaskill, Jr. You have got to remember that this is Cedar Island and not New York or San Francisco where they are used to these kinds of things. The minister who officiated at the funeral was the one who had been counseling Wain in Raleigh. The church was packed to overflowing with these tough, seasoned fishermen, dressed in their finest. No one quite knew what to expect, but the tone was set from the outset.

The minister rose, and the first words out of his mouth were, "Gerald Wain Gaskill, Jr. was gay, and he died from AIDS, but if that is all you remember about today and his life, then you have missed the point of his living." Well, you could have heard a feather drop in the church. Eyes became immediately red, and everyone was touched when Wain's father, Jerry, got up and read Wain's favorite Robert Frost poem:

The Road Not Taken
Two roads diverged in a yellow wood,
And sorry I could not travel both
And be one traveler, long I stood
And looked down one as far as I could
To where it bent in the undergrowth;

Then took the other, as just as fair,
And having perhaps the better claim,
Because it was grassy and wanted wear;
Though as for that the passing there

Had worn them really about the same.

And both that morning equally lay
In leaves no step had trodden black.
Oh, I kept the first for another day!
Yet knowing how way leads on to way,
I doubted if I should ever come back.

I shall be telling this with a sigh
Somewhere ages and ages hence:
Two roads diverged in a wood, and I—
I took the one less travelled by,
And that has made all the difference.

    I was sitting in the back row not wanting to intrude on the family and people who had known Wain better than I. So it was easy to see everyone clearly as they emerged from the church. What I saw moved me more than anything else in my life. Here were these weather-worn sailors and seamen, whose lives had been harder than any of us city dwellers can possibly imagine—people who I expected to be derisive about Wain and his choices in life, emerging from the church with red, tear-stained faces and embracing the family with genuine affection and sorrow. I made my comments to Jerry and Charran and left, for I had a six-hour drive back home. But one thing I concluded, Gerald Wain Gaskill, Jr.'s life was certainly not lived in vain. The people who he touched that day will never forget him. I wished that I had known Gerald Wain Gaskill, Jr. better during his life.

The Dedicated Guide

    A couple of years ago, Charlene and I were hunting, and the second day promised sleeting rain and bitter cold with the prospect of changing to snow and ice. We debated on whether to call it quits after the first day and just come on home but decided against it.

    At dinner that night, Jerry told us that almost everyone was leaving, but since we were staying, he was going to have Mike Austin put us in a marsh blind on the back side of the bay from Jerry's house. Jerry said that we could kill all the buffleheads we wanted and maybe get a mallard or a redhead or two. They would all be coming into the bay when the storm hit.

    He said that it was an area where we could not wade, and if the wind was at our backs, Mike would stay with us and retrieve ducks as long as we wanted to hunt.

    Mike is relatively new to the motel business. He was once a fisherman and may still do a little of it. However, when Ed Gaskill died, Jerry needed some help, and Mike was there. Mike is typical of the other fishermen at Cedar Island: tough, but with a little more polish—and that helps since he has to deal with the public all day. On this occasion, he really earned his keep.

    We left from the dock before six in a drizzle, and it was quite cold. It was a short run across the bay, and soon we were set up in a brush blind with little protection from the wind. Mike moved down the bay about 200 yards and hid his boat in a small cut in the marsh. He had told me that when we knocked something down, to give him a wave, and he would come pick it up.

    We had barely gotten situated and had our guns loaded when here came the first of many flights of buffleheads. With the storm brewing, the little buggers, affectionately known as "buffalo-brains" and "dippers," began swooping in on us in droves. We downed three or four in the first flight and waved to Mike. He immediately came and picked them up, but before he could return to his haven, we were shooting again, and he had to turn around and pick up more.

This went on all morning, and the weather kept getting worse and worse. We could not keep anything dry. I believe Mike made about 12 or 15 trips from his little cut before 10:00 am, at which time we decided we had better go in and get packed. If we stayed all day, we might be iced in overnight and not be able to drive in the morning. I won't tell you how many buffleheads we took in that morning, but I will say two things about that day: Mike was dedicated beyond the call of duty, and we had enough buffleheads for many stews for the rest of the winter.

Traditions

Some of this has already been discussed, but it can stand repeating. Over the years, we have developed some time-honored traditions, which I am convinced if we did not follow, the trip would simply not be a successful one.

First, you have to have the right gear, and packing for a Cedar Island trip is just about as much fun as going on the trip itself. Here are some things that are absolute musts: two Coleman catalytic heaters (never know how cold it might be), a large Igloo cooler (to bring home your ducks, hopefully one of Marcel's incomparable lemon pies, and occasionally, several bushels of oysters or clams), two sets of Duofold long underwear, one set of Thinsulate long underwear, down outer pants (in case it gets really cold), a scarf, two or three pairs of gloves, rubber gloves for retrieving the ducks and helping to pick up decoys at the end of the day, two Gore-tex heavy jackets, a down vest, Gore-tex watch caps (regular caps get in the way in case you want to put up the hood on your big jacket to keep off the wind or rain), two sets of waders (preferably neoprene for comfort and two in case one gets ripped), four or five pairs of socks (preferably the 90% wool variety, which are difficult to find), sunglasses, chapstick, at least two flashlights (a big one and a mini-mag for scrounging around the blind in the dark or trying to find your gear in the boat when you are trying to unload), a good, reliable pair of binoculars, Kleenex or toilet paper, a couple of thermoses (for soup and orange juice), and a spoon (how else are you going to eat your beanee weanies and pudding?).

That's just the gear—now to the food. Jerry's lunches, although significantly improved over the years, still leave a lot to be desired. When you are sitting in a cold, wet blind all day, you need some hot food. An absolute must are

Wranglers (a spicy hot dog made by Hormel)—at least three per person are required for a full day—mustard and buns for the Wranglers, six or eight bite-size candy bars per person (after all, we have to keep our energy level up, don't we?), two or three soft drinks per person, one or two bottles of V-8 juice per person, two pieces of Kentucky Fried Chicken per person, an orange or an apple apiece, a thermos of hot Swanson chicken broth, a thermos of cold orange juice (preferably fresh and not from concentrate), a couple of bags of potato chips to go with the Wranglers, and some Royal oatmeal cookies round out our day's supply of goodies.

    The travel tradition goes something like this. We try to leave about 8:00 or 9:00 am in order to time our arrival in Kinston about 11:00 am so we can eat at King's BBQ. King's serves excellent barbeque and home-cooked vegetables—a great stop in the trip. One of the primary reasons to stop is that Neuse Sporting Goods Store is next door, and not stopping at Neuse would be like a day without sunshine. We don't usually buy anything there, but it has become a tradition that must be preserved. After a good lunch at King's, it's on to Havelock for our next stop at the Kentucky Fried Chicken outlet on Highway 100 across from Cherry Point Marine Airbase. Here we buy enough chicken breasts for each person in the party. The last stop is at Jerry's store at the motel for a couple of bags of ice. We put our drinks, chicken, Wranglers, candy bars, and orange juice in the cooler the whole time we are there, and they stay fresh.

    Yes, there is a room ritual. Once arrived, we organize the room according to who is sleeping where. Underwear is laid out for the next morning, along with socks, vests, waders, scarves, and hats. All Wranglers are wrapped in tin foil, and buns are wrapped two to a package. Shell cases are checked and heaters filled with fuel. We are now ready either to walk on the beach before dinner or just to relax with a nap until about 6:30 when we head to the restaurant for our first "downeast seafood dinner."

Breakfast is served at 5:15 am, but we have learned that it is best to get there about 4:45 and get the table where you can see the food being brought from the kitchen. This allows you to be first in line for breakfast, to be first back to your room, a chance for a potty stop, and to be first to the dock for prime seating on the boat and prime spots for loading gear in the boat. You see, there is a methodology to this madness.

Before we leave for breakfast, we get the soup going about 4:30 when we get up. That way, the thermos is ready even before we leave for breakfast, and all we have to pack up when we return is anything we might want to take with us from Jerry's lunch. The Wranglers, soft drinks, orange juice, buns, candy bars, potato chips, mustard, fruit, etc. are packed before while we are preparing to go to breakfast.

After breakfast, we finish our packing—get on our waders and outer gear, load the car, and are off.

Dressing has a ritual too. Underwear is followed by the first set of Duofold long underwear. Then the first pair of socks go on and are taped with masking tape to the long underwear. If you don't do this, by the end of the day, those socks have eaten their way down into your waders, and you can hardly walk—that is very uncomfortable.

Next the Thinsulate underwear goes on, and another pair of socks goes on and is taped. As an aside, a little tip about taping—when taping socks, if you fold under the last one inch of tape, you will have something to grab onto to pull the tape off at the end of the day—if you don't do this, you had better have long fingernails, because after a day of that tape setting and with the moisture that accumulates inside the waders, it becomes almost impossible to get off.

Then come the tops (both sets of long underwear), and now you are ready to go to breakfast.

When you return, the last pair of socks goes on, then the waders, the vest, the scarf, and finally the outer jacket, hat, and gloves—and man, you are now ready for anything that might come along.

There is a ritual on the trip home; however, it is not as complex. The main thing is to time your trip so you arrive in Goldsboro about noon so you can eat at Wilbur's BBQ and get some of his banana pudding. Another stop at Neuse in Kinston is in order, and the rest of the trip is usually conversation about what a wonderful time was had.

One other thing that is not a ritual, but if you are lucky and can find someone selling some collard greens, or you can cut them yourself, bring home a car load—no better eating in the world!

But I Thought That Was a Legitimate Duck!

All of the "authorities" who supposedly control duck hunting advocate that you need to identify the duck while it is flying before you shoot at it. This is in order to ensure that you are not shooting something that is an endangered species or something that is outlawed.

There are a couple of problems with this. First, I defy anyone to accurately and consistently identify ducks flying at about 50 to 60 miles an hour, coming out of seemingly nowhere, before grabbing a gun and jumping up to shoot. Some are more identifiable than others, but, for example, I do not think it is possible to tell the difference between a redhead, a bluebill, or even a mallard flying that fast at distances of 100 or more yards on a foggy or rainy day—and that assumes there is no following wind, which increases the duck's flying speed to about 80 miles per hour.

Secondly, when you first begin duck hunting, you are lucky to be able to tell the difference between a bufflehead and a pintail when first exposed to them. And anyone who has hunted at Cedar Island, even an experienced person, will have trouble telling the difference between a cormorant and a Canada goose until it is upon you and you are about to pull the trigger (unless you can hear the geese calling to each other). The point of this is that even the best of hunters are occasionally going to down an illegal duck, and then the question becomes what to do with it.

Well, this is not an ethical treatise, so I'll stop here and just tell you some strange experiences I have had, which to animal lovers will be considered intolerable, but anyone who has hunted will find them understandable.

Early in my hunting experience at Cedar Island, we were in a marsh blind, and Charlene and I noticed this huge duck, which we could not identify, swimming around at the far end of the little pond in front of our marsh blind. Even with binoculars, we were not sure what it was because it kept darting in and out of the little cuts off the marsh bank.

Since it did not seem to want to come anywhere near us, I decided that I had better leave the blind and try to sneak up on it and maybe get a shot. I crept slowly around the edge of the marsh, and soon, when I raised up over the marsh grass, there it sat happily feeding.

I jumped up, hoping it would take off so I wouldn't have to shoot it on the water, but it refused to move. I assumed that maybe it had already been shot and was wounded, so I went ahead and shot. It immediately went belly up.

It was a beautiful bird, one worth mounting, and I was quite proud of my quarry as I came back to the blind. Charlene admired it too, and we immediately took out our duck identification booklet to try to determine what it was—unfortunately, we could not find it in there and had no choice but to wait on James for an identification.

Shortly, James pulled up to check on us, and I proudly displayed this unidentified bird for his professional scrutiny. He took one look and threw the duck as far into the marsh as he could and said, "Load up your gear and let's get out of here quickly!" We did not question his judgment—all we knew is that we had done something wrong and needed to leave in case a wildlife officer came by and found us in possession of this bird. As we left, James said that we had shot a Loon and it was a $500 fine, and the wildlife man could confiscate our guns and equipment, and even James' boat if he wanted to if he found us with the bird.

I felt really badly about this and vowed that from now on, I was going to be a better student of waterfowl.

On another occasion during our early hunts, redheads were off-limits. They seemed to fill the skies as is the case when there is a bird you cannot shoot. They are beautiful birds, particularly the males. They are somehow related to mallards and bluebills and fly in identical patterns when flying in singles or doubles. However, when they fly as huge flocks, they alter their flying patterns and fly "ups and downs," as though they are demented, or at best have no concept of where they are going or how they are going to get there.

It is relatively easy to identify redheads when they are flying in large flocks because of their "crazy" flying patterns, but, as I said, when flying in singles or even in pairs, it is almost impossible to tell the difference in them and mallards or bluebills, unless the sun just happens to hit their red heads as they fly by. Then you can pull up and not shoot.

In the early days, some of the guides made fatal assumptions that all the duck hunters who came to Cedar Island were equally knowledgeable about what could be shot and what could not be shot. James failed to tell us that first or second time down that redheads were off limits.

On this particular day, Charlene and I had about three or four beautiful male redheads in the blind when James came to check on us, and he about wet his pants when he saw them. He immediately put them under the floorboards of his boat and said that he would try to get them cleaned for us but to not shoot any more if we could help it. He said that if he saw a wildlife man, he would have to dispose of them and give the coons on the Outer Banks a good meal. I really hated to hear that but felt worse that we did it innocently.

No matter how careful you are, when a huge flock of 200 to 300 birds flies over you, all mixed up together, which happens sometimes, it is impossible to just pick out the valid ducks and shoot at them. After all, even if you could pick out the acceptable ones, no one can consistently shoot that accurately. Occasionally, we would kill something we shouldn't and would have to let it drift away. That is a sad sight.

If there is a moral to this story, I guess it is first, to know your ducks as well as possible and practice identifying them on the wing before shooting, and second, it is probably best to not shoot at all if you are unsure. If people keep killing ducks they are not supposed to shoot, pretty soon, there won't be any hunting for any of us anymore.

Do Sea Gulls Like Alka-Seltzer?

The answer is "No!" But sometimes it is necessary to enhance their normal diet with a few Alka-Seltzers.

This does not aid their digestive system, and we are not doing this on behalf of the Sierra Club or the Audubon Society.

Everyone knows that sea gulls are scavengers and will literally eat anything. This is why they are on the protected species list, because they do perform a service of cleaning up our oceans and estuaries. But sometimes, they can be a real menace to duck hunters.

Once, we were in a marsh blind where wading was impossible because of the depth of the bay. The wind was blowing out across the bay, and every time we would down a duck, it would float away from us across the bay. After a while, you couldn't even see them anymore. We tried to keep track of them so when the guide came, he could go to the other side of the bay and retrieve the ducks we had shot.

A major problem arose that interfered with this well thought out plan. As ducks would drift beyond our decoys about 100 yards, the sea gulls would begin to swoop down and start to pick out their breasts.

Dead ducks usually float belly up, and this was a real treat for the sea gulls—a dinner they didn't have to work too hard for. We couldn't shoot the sea gulls, although that was about as tempted as I had ever been to put a few of them into the water. Something had to be done or pretty soon, we would have nothing to take home for ourselves—the gulls were coming in batches by now. If we couldn't stop them, it would be pointless to keep shooting because all we were doing was feeding the sea gulls, and they had enough to eat anyway.

I had heard of this remedy somewhere but had never tried it.

I took out a bottle of Alka-Seltzer and started throwing the pellets as far as I could. As soon as they would hit the water, they would start to fizzle and disintegrate. Apparently, this fizzle attracted the sea gulls—after all, here was a treat they had never seen before. Immediately, they began attacking the Alka-Seltzer. They gobbled it up as fast as we could throw it and soon forgot about the ducks.

Then a funny thing happened. The gulls couldn't digest the pellets but did not want to let them go. Pretty soon, they were flying all around us, dripping fizzling Alka-Seltzer and looking like flying mad dogs. I guess it turned them off of the location because pretty soon, there were no sea gulls to be found anywhere, and our ducks were safe.

Now, I don't go to the blind without a large bottle of Alka-Seltzer—the newest innovation in sea gull repellent. I suppose it is okay to feed the sea gulls; however, I would prefer to take my delicious redheads, pintails, and mallards home for my enjoyment. After all, I do not get them as frequently as the sea gulls do!

Floating Seats and Other Duck Blind Discomforts

Most of the blinds at Cedar Island are stilt blinds built several feet up over the sound, and they stay relatively dry, even in downpours, because other thoughtful hunters, or the guides who built them, have blown drain holes in the bottom (unless you are unfortunate enough to inherit one of Newt's former blinds, and then you had better check the structural damage before the guide leaves, or you may be standing in three feet of water for several hours through no fault of your own).

Marsh blinds are not always that protected. I have heard conflicting stories about tides in Core Sound. Some people have told me that the water level in the sound is not affected by tides because the entire sound is protected by the barrier islands of the Outer Banks. Others disagree, and swear that tides do affect the water level. I tend to accept the latter opinion, and here is my proof.

We were having a slow day on the Banks, and James decided to move us into the marsh for the afternoon. It had been raining hard the past few days, and James said that we were "having high tides" so it would be no trouble to get into the marsh (sometimes the water is so low you cannot get a boat to some of the blinds).

We roared into the marsh, and it quickly became apparent that the shoreline was not very discernable. It really looked strange because usually there is about a foot drop-off from the marsh to the water. Today, it all seemed to blend together.

When James pulled up to the blind and we stepped out, we stepped onto the marsh bank, and water was already up to our knees. The sides of these marsh blinds are not wooden; they are just scrub bushes piled up, and the seats are inverted fish boxes as opposed to the planks we sit on in the stilt blinds.

As we stepped into the blind, our "seats" were floating around. James took a look and said, "Don't worry, when you sit on them, they won't float!" Well, he was correct about that, but what he didn't mention is that when we stood up to shoot, our seats would start mysteriously floating around the blind, and if you weren't careful, they would either bump you over into the bushes or they wouldn't be there when you went to sit down.

This created other problems as well. Where do you store your gun, your heater, your gear bag, and all the other little sundries we must have with us? Well, we held our guns on our laps and placed our back-up guns in the bushes next to us out of the water. We hung our gear bags on sturdy branches and searched out another old fish box and turned it tall-side up and put our heater on it. "Necessity," the one from the quote, "Necessity is the mother of invention," must have been first thought of in a Cedar Island marsh blind during high tide, because if you weren't inventive, you could not hunt there.

The only tragedy of the day was that I dropped an expensive pair of Nikon binoculars into the foot-deep water that surrounded us. I was able to retrieve them, but they were never the same again. We overcame adversity, as you must do if you are going to succeed, and had a marvelous afternoon of bluebill shooting.

The Stalk

Sometimes, you have to go to the ducks—they don't always come to you. On two occasions, I had to stealthily stalk my quarry because they just did not want to fly.

We used to frequently hunt a little known creek named Oyster Creek when the bluebills were at Cedar Island because this was one of their favorite haunts. I don't know what particularly attracted them to this little creek, but when "they were in town," they would flock to it in droves. We were hunting out of another marsh blind about 300 yards away from Oyster Creek, and it was a dull day. Nothing was flying. When this happens, and I am in the marsh, I always opt for a walk because there are always little mysteries of the marsh to explore. Occasionally, you will find the wild ponies that inhabit the marshes around Cedar Island.

The story is that some farmer brought them to Cedar Island to raise and sell, but there was not much of a market for them, and he let them go. They drifted away from the main island and made a new home on the marshes out in Core Sound. Since they drifted there years ago, storms and man-made ditches have cut them off from the mainland.

Now they live out their lives in the marshes. Don't feel sorry for them for there is plenty to eat, people leave them alone except for the occasional hunter who visits them, and there is even a freshwater spring in the middle of the marsh "where they hang out," so they have fresh water when they need it.

Anyway, on this day, I told Charlene that I was going to hike over to Oyster Creek—not an easy trip because it is all through sawgrass, and you know how I feel about sawgrass. However, the ponies and other critters that live in the marsh have made little winding paths through this sawgrass, and, if you are careful and don't mind spending a little extra time, you can go about where you want to with little walking difficulty.

No one was hunting Oyster Creek these days because the bluebills were not at the sound this year, and none of the guides had even put up blinds along the creek. I didn't really expect to find anything, but I was bored, and it was a good excuse to stretch my legs. Even though I didn't expect to find any ducks puddling around, anytime you start walking around the marsh, you had better be prepared because just when you expect to find nothing, a duck or two will surprise you from one of the many potholes and be gone before you can shoot.

I knew I had a long way to go to Oyster Creek, but I took my time because there are numerous potholes along the way. And who knows? Maybe a stray redhead or mallard might just be quietly feeding in one of them. Nothing jumped up as I walked, and I was about 100 yards from the creek when I thought that I saw something in the water that was barely visible above the top of the sawgrass. I knelt down and took out my binoculars. Slowly, I got up just above the sawgrass and looked at the creek.

Wow!—There were at least 10 or 12 ducks right in the middle of the creek—just sitting there, and they hadn't seen me yet. I immediately got down and started planning my approach.

Ducks, even when not threatened, are very wary creatures. I knew if they saw the tops of the sawgrasses moving, they would be spooked and would fly before I could get anywhere near them. The only safe plan was to crawl slowly and quietly through the sawgrass until I was about 30 yards away. Then I could afford to get up and shoot. Boy, was that a job. Not only is that stuff thick, the short grasses are like needles, and 100 yards on your knees can take it out of an Olympic athlete.

It must have taken over an hour to get close. Every few yards, I would creep up and take another look, and sure enough, they were exactly where I had seen them before—they didn't appear to have moved an inch. Boy!—What luck! I crept on.

By the time I was close enough to chance a shot, I had torn a hole in my $100 waders. Well, I thought, that's okay—it will be worth it to take about four or five ducks back to the blind on such a slow day.

Finally, I was in a position to shoot, and I decided the best plan was to take the safety off first, get up quickly, and get off three quick shots because they would be long gone before I could reload.

I jumped up and started to pull the trigger and something strange happened. They did not move a feather! I yelled at them to fly, and still they stared at me as though I were were some kind of apparition. Then it dawned on me—they were looking at me through plastic eyes—these damn ducks I had wasted two or three hours on were decoys, firmly anchored to the bottom. No one can fully understand the term "feeling foolish" until you have done something like this.

I felt so dumb, I was embarrassed to walk back to the blind and have to tell Charlene what I had done. I guess we see what we want to see, and that day, I saw Oyster Creek come to life again—but it was only a figment of my imagination.

An equally embarrassing experience happened when I was hunting with Charlie on the Banks one day. Again, it was a slow day, and I asked him if he wanted to hike to the Banks. He declined because his knee was bothering him.

All day, I had been looking at three or four ducks sitting behind us near an unoccupied blind. They were four or five hundred yards away, and it was impossible to wade near enough to them to get a shot. Besides, it was probably too deep to get there anyway. Yet I kept thinking, "If I walked to the Banks, I could walk down the shore and back out to where they were and maybe get a shot." They were facing away from the Banks, and if I was careful, maybe I could sneak up close enough to get a shot without them seeing me. They had not flown all morning—they had just sat there staring out into the sound.

Loaded with shells and determined to bring back some quarry, off I trudged through the shallow water toward the Banks. It only took about 30 minutes to get to the Banks' shoreline, and I took out my binoculars, and yep, they were still sitting there. This was my opportunity. We had only killed about two ducks all day, and it was already about 2:30 in the afternoon. Only a couple more hours before we were to be picked up, and nothing in sight except these ducks that had been defying us all day.

Ever so quietly, I casually walked down the marsh line until I was directly in line with these ducks sitting about 300 yards out into the sound. Like Garfield sneaking up on Odie, I carefully took one quiet step after another. The ducks never even turned to look at me.

I got within 50 yards of them, and since I was carrying my 12 gauge, three inch magnum, I felt I could get one or two from here and was afraid to chance going any further. The wind was in my face, and if I spooked them, they would take off into the wind away from me, and I would lose my chance forever.

Carefully, I raised the gun, took dead aim, and fired a round. Nothing happened, but I saw the shot spray the water all around them. Quickly, I got off two more shots, and they covered those ducks—no way I could have missed—but they did not fly. I was sure I had hit them. I picked up my pace and hurried toward them. Suddenly, I had this sinking feeling—something like, "I wonder if I have just killed some more decoys?"

You guessed it! I had peppered three of somebody's decoys pretty good. Embarrassed, I turned around and headed back to the blind, wondering what kind of ribbing I was going to get from Charlie when I got back. Surely he had heard the shooting, and he had binoculars. He would wonder why I killed some ducks and then didn't pick them up. I wondered if he would believe that they were trash ducks I really didn't want, or maybe I could tell him they were off-limits ducks, and I did not know that until I had shot. But then he would probably wonder why I had not gone all the way to look at them before rejecting them. Maybe I could tell him that I looked at them through the binoculars and saw they were illegal and that is why I didn't go to get them.

All of this ran through my mind, and by the time I got back, I had decided to just tell the truth and let him have a good laugh and forget about it. When I got back, Charlie was sound asleep. When I awoke him, all he said was, "Did you have a good hike?" I replied, "Yes," and nothing more was said. I wonder if he knew and was just being polite.

Anyway, when he reads this, he will know the truth, and next year, I guess he will find an opportunity to ask me if I want to go on a hike and shoot some decoys.

If You Have a Dog, Leave Him at Home!

Labs, goldens, and Chesapeake Bay retrievers are wonderful duck dogs and have a place in duck hunting, but not at Cedar Island.

People who own these dogs are very devoted to them, and duck hunting without their favorite lab, golden, or whatever just wouldn't be the same. But at Cedar Island, it is a different story. I have often thought of suggesting to Jerry that in his annual announcement letter about the coming season, he ought to suggest to hunters that retrievers are just not appropriate at Cedar Island and to leave them at home.

First, it is not my place to tell him how to run his business, and second, if he did that, he might lose some business that he otherwise would have.

The problem is that dogs at Cedar Island can cause havoc, not only for the owner, but for those in blinds around him. Let me explain.

For a retriever to really be effective, he must be able to see the duck fall; otherwise, he has no idea where to swim to retrieve the downed bird. Since in all the stilt blinds, it is impossible for the dog to see out, he has no concept of where to go when the owner shoots, throws open the door, and tells "Rover" to fetch. Poor Rover might swim about for an hour trying to find a duck among the 50 or 60 decoys that are out there. In the meantime, he will spook any other ducks trying to fly by.

Then there comes the problem of trying to get this 100 pound animal back into the blind. He is wet, he can't get his feet on the poles that are used for steps, and the real problem is that the poor dog can get worn out and drown or have a heart attack trying to do what his unthinking master expects of him. This means that the owner has to get out of the blind, try to pick up 100 pounds of struggling, wet, tired animal, and hoist him up five or six feet into the blind. Come to think of it, both of them could have a heart attack.

And, not to be underestimated, there is the problem of normal bodily discharges that are bound to overcome this dog while spending 10 or 12 hours in a blind. Now what do you do with a dog that is as big as you are when he has "to go" and there is no place "to go?" "Well, he damn sure ain't gonna 'go' on my feet and me have to sit in it all day!" Beginning to see the problem?

There is another not so small problem with dogs. They get bored. These dogs are born and trained for action. If they see their master get up and shoot, they have been trained to "move and retrieve." Further, they love the water and can't wait to get in.

Back in the days when the "clouds of ducks" were at Cedar Island and shooting was an all-day affair, Charlie and I found ourselves about 200 yards away from a blind with two hunters and a dog in it. We could hear that blasted dog barking all day. Needless to say, these hunters did not get much shooting that day because it seemed that anytime ducks started heading for their blind, the dog would bark for some unknown reason (it sure wasn't because he could see them because he couldn't—we suspect it was out of uncontrollable boredom).

This actually was working to our advantage because as the ducks would approach their blind, the dog would bark, diverting the ducks around that blind, and then they would form up again and head straight for us. We shot all day.

It was about 3:00 in the afternoon, just as the returning flights were beginning to come in, and we were excited about the final two hours of shooting about to happen. Just then, we saw the dog bolt from the other blind. He wasn't chasing anything because there was nothing to chase. I suspect that he was simply bored out of his mind and saw a chance to escape and have a little fun, and he took advantage of the situation. It would have been funny except for what happened next.

Rover would not respond to his owner's call to return. Can you blame him? Poor devil had been cooped up in that 4x6 foot box since shortly after 6:00 am—hadn't retrieved a duck all day—and was sick of it, his master, the cramped quarters, and, by now, probably the smell as well.

Off he went, barking and swimming and romping around having the time of his life. Finally, his master got out of the blind and started after him. Well this was futile. The dog was having no part of getting back into that blind and led his owner on a merry chase for about an hour and a half.

It was funny at first, and we were laughing at the stupidity of the owner until we realized that the ducks were flaring all around both our blinds because of the commotion. It was then that I believe had not Charlie been a "sworn police officer and defender of the right" that he would have cheerfully shot both man and beast. Well, it ruined our afternoon, and maybe now you will agree with me that retrievers are best left at home for hunts at Cedar Island.

While they may be wonderful in blinds at the lake, they cannot function in stilt blinds where they are literally blinded from doing what they have been trained to do.

Stand-Uppers Are Okay—As Long as You Are Not One of Them

Guides cannot think of everything to tell hunters, particularly those new to hunting at Cedar Island. But one thing you learn quickly is that there is a reason for the little peep holes and slits judiciously cut near the tops of the blinds and in appropriate places throughout the blind walls. They are for looking through so you can see ducks coming before they can see you.

Some people don't know that, and they will stand up all day long looking out toward the horizon for incoming ducks. What they do not seem to understand is that ducks have 10 power plus vision and can see you long before you can see them.

Ducks are used to the box blinds used at Cedar Island because they see them being built. When they see one or two objects sticking about three feet above the top of these boxes, they know that something is amiss, and it is a signal to avoid that box.

One time, Dick Whittington and I were hunting together, and just about all the blinds along the Banks had hunters in them. It was a busy time at Cedar Island, and even though I had rather hunt in a blind away from everyone else because of dogs and "sky-busters," sometimes you don't have a choice.

The nearest blind to us was about 200 yards away and was occupied by "stand-uppers." Now, these were not ordinary "stand-uppers." They stood up back to back the entire day. Every now and then, you will see people standing up when no flying is occuring, just to stretch out the kinks of sitting so long. But these clowns stood back to back for 10 straight hours—I honestly do not believe they sat down for more than a minute or two at at time—and when one sat, the other remained on vigil.

I commented to Dick that when James came, we ought to send him over there and tell them how this business works so they could enjoy the day more. But something was happening that we didn't realize at first. We were shooting and they were not.

What was happening was that as ducks approached their blind, they saw these two idiots standing up, and they flared away from them and right at us. When we realized that, we decided, selfishly, I must admit, that we would keep our collective mouths shut and would never criticize "stand-uppers" again.

We didn't realize it until we got ready to go in that these two dumb heads were part of our boat party and we were going to ride in with them. When we got in, we asked them how their day had gone (as if we didn't know). One of them replied, "Well, we didn't do so good, but boy, you guys sure had a good day—we watched you knock 'em down all day!"

No shit, Sherlock!

Jerry's Infamous Lunches

I hope to give Jerry a copy of these "memoirs" if I ever finish them, but I might decline because I don't think he will appreciate this story very much. However, he knows it is true.

In the early days of Cedar Island duck hunting, the lunches we were given were something like you might expect if you had been exiled to a prison island for some cruel and horrendous act. We were all convinced, although I am sure this was not true, that they were made up sometime during the previous century and were, in fact, the very lunches served to the rowers on the old longboats that traversed these waters in the days of Treasure Island. Remember that these rowers were prisoners and deserved no better fare.

We used to get a couple of sandwiches, a piece or two of chicken if we were lucky, a piece of fruit (again, if we were lucky), and something that resembled a chocolate cookie, which with the first bite would immediately suck all of the saliva out of your mouth for the rest of the day—Boy! Were they dry!

The filling on the sandwiches was microscopically thin—thinner even than the towels in the motel—and you can easily read the newspaper through Jerry's towels. There was usually a pimento cheese sandwich, which gave us the most mammoth case of indigestion you can imagine, and then there was the mystery meat sandwich. My oldest daughter, Mary, was a student at Elon College, and occasionally, we used to ask her about the food served there. She used to always talk about the "mystery meat," but I really didn't know what she meant until I sampled some of Jerry's sandwich creations. This meat resembled nothing you have ever seen and did not appear edible. In fact, on more occasions than not, we fed them to the sea gulls, hoping they would get sick and leave us alone. Even the sea gulls shunned them, and they are scavengers.

Sometimes there would be a styrofoam container of macaroni salad. Nobody I know was brave enough to eat that, and it was always the first thing that hit the sound. Maybe the macaroni salad is the cause of the dwindling supply of coons and other critters in the surrounding marshes. Anyone eating that stuff did not have long to live.

The fried chicken was the only thing palatable in the lunches, but we didn't always get fried chicken.

In fact, these lunches were what spurred Charlene and Charlie and I to create the Wrangler, Kentucky Fried Chicken, hot soup, etc. lunches we enjoy today.

To Jerry's credit, he conducted a survey a few years ago, and I had the privilege of working on it with him and tabulating the results. The only item where the hunting package at Cedar Island was rated low was the lunches. And again, to Jerry's credit, he listened.

The lunches today are 100% better, but they don't beat the hot Wranglers, hot soup, hot chicken, V-8 juice, candy bars, Beanee Weanies, and the other goodies that we now bring to the blind.

The Unplugged Gun

This is a story I swore Charlie to secrecy about and one I swore I would never tell on myself, but what the heck—these are memoirs, aren't they? And therefore, it comes with warts and all.

Just this last season, our 13th at the coast, Charlie and I were hunting together. Long ago, we realized it was good practice to take two guns apiece, just in case one jams or malfunctions. There have been times when a spring would come loose or something would happen to one gun, and it was nice to have a back up.

On our second day of hunting, Jerry told us to be careful that day because the game wardens were spending the night at the motel and would probably be checking up randomly on some of the blinds the next day. We normally don't concern ourselves with that because we are always careful to have our licenses and duck stamps with us at all times.

Another of the regulations is that in water fowling, your gun must be plugged for only three shots. This is for the purpose of giving the game a chance because all automatic shotguns are designed to hold one shell in the chamber and either four or five in the sleeve. This is because all sports do not limit the number of shots. For example, you can hunt pheasants, rabbits, squirrels, and other animals with the gun unplugged—but not waterfowl, and that is a federal, not a North Carolina, regulation.

I am partial to the old Browning A-5 shotguns. When I ordered my three inch magnum from Charlie, I checked it when it came and found it already had a plug installed from the factory. Therefore, years later when I ordered a two and three-quarter inch 12 gauge Browning A-5 from Charlie, I assumed it was also plugged. In fact, I had hunted with that gun at Cedar Island and other places for years and never checked it.

About 2:00 pm, we spotted "the man" at the blind next to us in his Boston Whaler checking on those hunters. He stayed there a long time, and we commented on the fact that he must have found something amiss and must be giving them a ticket.

Waterfowl violations can carry a very stiff penalty. Not only can they fine you, but if they are in a bad mood that day, they have the right to also confiscate your gear, guns, and even boats, in addition to giving you a fine. In other words, they can do about whatever they want. If they catch you over a baited blind (where corn has been strewn around on the bottom of the sound to attract ducks), you might as well hand it all over to them and go home because you are in deep s——! There is no mercy for that type of violation, nor should there be.

On this afternoon, we had no illegal ducks in the blind (not that we ever did, you understand), our licenses were intact, we both had our federal duck stamps—nothing was amiss. Charlie asked me, "Are both your guns plugged?" "Of course," I thought! But then he decided he would check his just to make sure, and I decided maybe I had better do the same.

I tried to cram a third shell into the loading port on the three inch and it would only go about halfway, so I knew it was okay. Then I tried the two and three-quarter inch, and a shell slipped in easily. I looked at Charlie and asked, "Did you reload this after I shot a few minutes ago?" He replied that he did. My heart jumped into my throat. I tried another shell, thinking that Charlie must be mistaken. It easily went in, and I began to panic. I stood up and started ejecting all the shells that were in the gun. On the floor of the blind at my feet lay five, count 'em, five unspent shells. My two and three-quarter inch gun did not have a plug in it! "What the hell am I going to do?," I asked Charlie. The color had drained from his face. We both knew that if "the man" checked on us, one of the first things he would do would be to check the guns to see if he could get more than three shells into each gun. Well, he certainly would have no difficulty with my two and three-quarter inch 12 gauge.

We sat there for a moment looking at each other. It was too late to jerry rig some type of plug. Any old stick will do, but there was no stick to be found. Then Charlie had a solution. Case the gun and put it under our bench. If the warden asked for our guns, we would give him my three inch and Charlie's two guns and just not say anything about the other gun hidden under the bench behind the rest of our gear. At the other blind, he was just standing on the bow of his boat talking to the hunters, maybe he would not get into our blind and rummage around. It was our only hope.

We sat there, in panic, as he cranked up his engine and headed our way. Neither of us could say anything just thinking about the possible consequences. Besides, I have found that it is difficult to talk when your heart is in your throat.

Here he came and here we sat. When he got to within about 30 yards of our blind behind us, he kicked his motor into high gear and sped off north toward Portsmouth Island and out of sight in about 20 minutes.

We just sat there for a full 10 minutes without saying anything and then began a lot of nervous chatter and laughter.

Needless to say, the gun stayed cased the rest of the day, and as soon as I got home, I fashioned a plug from a dowel rod, and the gun is now safely plugged for future waterfowl hunting. The sad part is that I never once shot more times than I was legally allowed, and never even thought of cheating like that. Yet had I been caught with an unplugged gun, as they say, ignorance is no excuse, and I would have been fined and possibly lost one or both guns. I shudder to think about it, and you can bet it will never happen to me or anyone I hunt with. It's too scary, besides being against the law.

John Said, "Boy, This Is Like Shooting Sitting Ducks"

If you leave the dock on time in the mornings, it is possible to get into your blind way before sunrise. In fact, sometimes it is pitch black dark, and you need a flashlight just to stow your gear. One morning, John and I found ourselves in such a situation. Actually, it is an advantage, because the early morning flights are the best, and you want to be there as early as possible, settled down, and listening for the rush of wings and splash-down of ducks in your decoys.

We didn't have to wait long as the "whoosh" of wings swept by us in the dark, and we heard the tell-tale "splash, splash, splash" of ducks landing in or near our decoys.

Remember, it was pitch dark, and we kept peering out of the cracks and crevices trying to discern real ducks from decoys. I honestly could not see well enough to even count the decoys. That is usually the very first thing we do when we get into a blind. We count the decoys and note their position just in case something flies in. Then, if we see something swimming around where it is not supposed to be, we know then it's the real thing.

John was convinced he saw two ducks close together among the decoys and wanted to shoot. I cautioned him to be absolutely sure, and he said, "I know they are real, Daddy, I can see them moving around." I had no idea what he was seeing, but since his eyes are about 25 years younger than mine, I said to go ahead and take a shot. We were in a brush blind in the marsh, and he eased his 12 gauge through an opening in the bushes, and "boom," the gun roared. He screamed, "I got them both—I got them both with one shot!" I said that was great, but let's wait until it is a little lighter and we will retrieve them.

The wind was blowing in our faces, so I knew that before long, they would drift up to the banks where our blind was, so there was no rush to get them. Besides, I didn't want to be out wading around in the dark just before other flights would be coming in.

It got uncharacteristically quiet for a while, and we just waited to see if others would come in as we gradually witnessed one of Cedar Island's famous sunrises. Streaks of colored light were just beginning to come across the sky, and I told John it was about time to get out and see if he could find his ducks. I told him they should be up against the bank by now so be sure to look under the lip of the marsh banks.

He was gone for what seemed like an awfully long time just to retrieve two ducks that were sure to be near the blind. A moment later, he came back empty-handed and said that he could not find them.

I muttered something about that being ridiculous, and we both set out to search for the ducks. He was right! They were nowhere to be found. As we walked back to the blind trying to figure out what had happened, I noticed that a couple of our decoys were sort of "listing to port." They did not look too well. In fact, they looked like they were about to sink.

I asked John where those two ducks he had shot had been sitting in relationship to the spread of decoys we had, and he pointed directly at the two malnutritioned ducks quickly going to the bottom of the pond. He barely got the words out of his mouth when he realized what had happened. We both started to laugh—John had killed his first pair of decoys, and he had done it with only one shot.

Now we had to decide what to do. We didn't want them to just sink because the guides know exactly how many decoys they put out and would know that we had shot a couple and didn't tell them. Decoys are expensive, and the guides don't make that much money out of this work.

John went wading for the wounded decoys, and we hid them behind the blind. When James came to check on us, we didn't have the courage to tell him what we had done, but it seemed that he looked at the decoy spread an awfully long time as he was leaving—like something was wrong but he didn't quite know what it was. I told John that we would have to tell James, and John would just have to take the ribbing that was sure to come.

So when James returned to check on us again later in the day, we hauled out the two "holey" decoys and told him what had happened. He just laughed and told us we might be surprised how many of his decoys end up looking like that by the end of the season. He said he could patch them easily and they would live to decoy another day.

The nicest thing about the whole experience is that nothing was said at dinner that night. I guess James realized that if he ribbed John about the decoys, John might be embarrassed and might be uncomfortable about coming back to Cedar Island. James has a lot of smarts that I didn't know he had—but now I know differently. I guess raising two boys yourself helps you understand how sensitive they can be about some things.

I always appreciated the fact that this incident was never mentioned; it would have given everyone a laugh, but the damage to John might have been irreversible.

A Nice, Unexpected Touch

At the end of a long, cold, windy day on the sound duck hunting, about all you are interested in is a long, hot shower and some of Jerry's excellent seafood. But one evening, we had a most pleasant surprise.

We were a bit late coming in that evening because James had to stop for some gas. I never minded when he had to do that because it meant that we didn't have to stop in the morning and could go roaring out in the sound when some of the other guides were lined up for gasoline. So we were a little later than normal getting to the room, and all I could think about was if there would be enough hot water for Charlie and me since everyone else had a head start.

As we rounded the back of the motel, I noticed a large crowd right beside our room, and they were all still dressed for hunting. I could not imagine what in the world was going on.

When we got out of the car, Jerry yelled, "Horace! Charlie! Come over and have some fresh oysters!" Some of the guides, during their "down time" that day, had been sent out by Jerry to harvest several bushels of oysters. Now Jerry and the guides were shucking oysters and handing them to us as fast as we could eat them.

First, a large cup of cocktail sauce was thrust into my hands, and then Jerry held up a fat oyster by the end of his oyster blade and shoved it into my mouth. No sooner had I consumed that one than here came another one from a different direction from another guide. What great eating—fresh oysters not an hour or two from the bays and sounds. Standing there in all our hunting clothes and eating fresh oysters shucked by the guides—I forgot all about the shower.

Jokes were being told, the day was being discussed, ducks downed were being talked about, and we were eating fresh oysters as fast as they could be offered. As the commercial says, "It don't get any better than this." What a great way to end the day, and what a thoughtful thing for them to do. There seems to be no end to the hospitality offered by Jerry and his staff to his hunting friends, and this is just further proof. If you haven't decided already that you should visit Cedar Island and become one of the group—this should convince you. It doesn't take long to get to know everyone, and you will make friends for life.

Watch Out for a Case of "Crack-Eye"

The wind "do blow at Cedar Island!" There have been very few days when I have not known the wind to whistle all around the blind, and sometimes, if you stand up just to stretch your legs, it is so brutal that you have to turn your back on it. This wind can play havoc, not only with your shooting leads and ability, but with your eyes as well. Let me explain.

As I have mentioned previously, each blind is so constructed that you have small slits or peep holes designed for you to look through in searching for ducks. If you stand up to look for them, you'll see plenty, but none will come close enough to shoot at because they will have seen you long before you see them. The idea is to stay down, even to the point where nothing on your person is above the horizontal top of the blind, and do your searching through these eye holes and slits.

Usually, hunting partners will divide up the search area. If I am sitting on the right side of the blind, I will be responsible for half the front, all of my side, and half of the back, and my partner assumes responsibility for the corresponding portions on his or her side. When the wind is blowing, it seems to concentrate itself with unusual velocity when it comes through these small openings. If you are doing your job, you are constantly watching out through these slits and holes, hoping for a glimpse of oncoming ducks so both hunters can have adequate time to prepare.

"Crack-eye" is a phrase coined by Charlie Maddry for that feeling at the end of the day where your eyes feel as though there are thousands of little tiny pins and needles under your eyelids. The only relief is to shut your eyes. Even then they sting, but that is the only relief you can get. It helps to wear glasses in the blind—they deflect some of the wind, but not all of it.

We have tried taping Saran Wrap on the outside of the blind to block the wind, but that cuts your visibility. In fact, we have not found an adequate solution to "crack-eye." You do not notice it during the day when you are out there. It is only at night when you come in, take your shower, observe your red, wind-burned face, and then realize that your eyes are stinging like crazy.

We have never tried any types of eye washes like Murine or Visine, but maybe that is a possible solution. We are open to any suggestions, because all the ones we have tried simply do not work. I am not sure any solution is really necessary because by the time you have hunted all day, had a hot shower, and eaten a full downeast seafood dinner, you can't keep your eyes open anyway.

But boy! What a wonderful feeling it is to tumble into bed and shut off those little pins and needles that have been poking around under your eyelids ever since you came in.

Nasal-Wik-a-Ways

One of the truly great inventions of all time was invented by my hunting partner, Charlie Maddry.

When it is cold and the wind blows, whether you have a cold or not, I can guarantee that your nose is going to "run" all day. In fact, that is why we always "steal" a roll of Jerry's toilet paper and stick it in our duck bag to take to the blind. Two people will easily use up more than half a full roll of toilet paper in the course of a cold, windy day.

During one of my hunts with Charlie, I noticed that he was continually reaching for the toilet paper and blowing his nose. Two minutes later, he was at it again, and by 10 or 11 o'clock, he looked like Rudolph, the Red-Nosed Reindeer. He had just about rubbed all the skin off his nose.

After a while, I realized that he had quit blowing his nose. You can be within a half mile of Charlie, and on a calm day, you can tell if he has quit blowing his nose. The only thing louder than a Maddry "blow" is a Maddry "snore," but that's another story. I looked over his way to see if he had just fallen asleep, and it was obvious he hadn't because his head was turned away from me as he scanned the horizon on his side of the blind. I said something like, "How's your nose? Haven't heard you rattle the blind's foundation lately."

When he turned around, I could see why, and it was one of the funniest sights I had ever seen. Here was this bundled up man, hat pulled down over his ears, scarf up around his neck and mouth, eyes behind dark glasses trying to avoid a massive dose of "crack-eye" with two three- or four-inch long rolled up slivers of toilet paper stuffed up each nostril. He looked like a beached walrus. I laughed until my sides hurt. I said, "What in the world are those for?"

He said, "These are my 'Nasal-Wik-a-Ways' because my nose is about to fall off, and if I keep blowing it, it will fall off!"

Well, laugh we did, but you know, they worked. For the rest of the day, both of us sat there, rolling up toilet paper into fine little tubes and stuffing them up our noses. When they would get a little "soppy," we would just pull them out, throw them away, and stuff some more up the ole snoot. Saves toilet paper and noses!

Now, if someone would just invent a similar homemade remedy for "crack-eye," we would have it made.

Charlene's First Shot

I am about to confess something that Charlene never knew. In fact, when she proofreads this, this particular story might be deleted (editor's privilege, you understand)—but worse, my marriage might be in jeopardy.

When I first invited Charlene to go to Cedar Island, I talked at length with Charlie about what type of gun to get her. We didn't want to spend the money for an automatic shotgun, even though the recoil would be less, and it would be a more pleasant gun to shoot because we didn't know if she would like hunting or not. If she hated it, then I would have wasted a lot of money for a two-day hunting trip.

We settled on a Stevens 20 gauge double barrel, and Charlie suggested we start her out on light field loads. She might not kill anything with those light loads, but at least she wouldn't be turned off the experience altogether by the severe recoil that magnum shells can give you.

When we got her the new gun, she and I went out around home here, and she shot it a few times. You've got to remember that Charlene is a real trooper, and if she thought the gun was a little harsh, she never mentioned it. We were careful to at least get a shotgun that was chambered for both two and three-quarter as well as three inch shells in case she got the "hang" of it and wanted a little more firepower later on. We could always switch to three inch magnum shells.

We got into the blind that morning, and the more I thought about it, the more I did not want her shooting those light field loads. She was a beginner, and we didn't expect great shooting anyway, but if she did hit a duck with those loads, it would just keep on flying as though a gust of wind had hit it.

While she was busy fiddling with her gear, I slipped in two three inch magnum shells. I figured that if she shot at something, she would be so excited at shooting at a live, moving target that she would not feel the recoil anyway.

It wasn't long before I was to put my theory to the test. A group of bluebills came in and sat in our decoys. I wanted Charlene to have an easy first shot to build up her confidence, so I suggested that she slip up and shoot one on the water. For Charlene to slip "up" and shoot one on the water is fraught with problems other than magnum shells.

Remember that the blinds are about four and a half feet tall from floor to ceiling and Charlene is barely five feet tall in hunting boots. To try and get the gun to her shoulder and then "shoot down" at sitting or landing ducks is virtually impossible for her. The ducks cooperated by not flying off as she tried two or three times to aim, but she just couldn't get the angle right.

I suggested that she sneak up and stand on her seat and then she would have plenty of room for the proper shooting angle. This worked great until she fired. In her excitement, even with a double trigger, she managed to pull off both shots simultaneously, and the next sequence of events seemed right out of a Laurel and Hardy movie.

Not expecting the recoil from one, much less two magnum shells, the jolt caused her to lose her balance, and she was slammed into the back of the blind. The noise and the recoil so shocked her that she dropped the shotgun into the blind, and the force broke the forearm of the stock off the Stevens (they were never very good guns anyway, if you ask me). I was afraid that she was going over the back of the blind into the water, and I scrambled to put my gun down, planning to try and catch her. Instead, she just crumpled into the corner of the blind and then to the floor.

When she looked up, all she said was, "Did I get one?" Is that a trooper or what?

She recovered and never said a word about the recoil. She seemed more concerned about her gun being broken, but I assured her that it would shoot just fine the way it was, and we finished out the day "on light field loads" with a broken shotgun.

Since she enjoyed the experience so much (not that particular incident, but the whole trip), her birthday present the next year was a new Remington 1100 20 gauge with a short, 22 inch barrel. She loves it and has become a pretty good shot with it. We still haven't solved the height problem, but most of the ducks we shoot at are in the air anyway, so at least she doesn't have to stand on the seat to get a good shot.

Fetch

One time, Charlene and I were hunting a marsh blind with the wind in our faces, which meant that anything we killed would float to the bank near us and would make retrieving a "piece of cake"—didn't even have to get into the water.

We were in the blind long before sunrise, and we could hear the bluebills whooshing in and landing all around us. The problem was, we couldn't see them. We couldn't even see the decoys that were as close as 20 yards in front of us.

What a maddening experience to know that you are surrounded by ducks and can't even see them, much less shoot at them. We waited as patiently as we could until the first crack of light and we could begin to distinguish moving forms in the water.

We need not have been too concerned about waiting because this was one of those mornings you dream about.

This was back in the days of a seven duck limit per hunter as long as two of the seven ducks were bluebills. We started shooting about 6:30, and by 7:05 am, the pond in front of us looked like the battlefield after Patton and Rommel went at each other at El Alamein. Ducks lay drifting everywhere. We had been shooting so fast that we had honestly lost count of how many we had killed. As fast as we would shoot and that flock would leave, another would descend on us, and we would be shooting again.

Charlene wanted some exercise, so she volunteered to "fetch" the ducks for us. As she would walk along, it seemed that she was bending down about every two or three seconds picking up another duck and laying it on the bank. I kept calling out to her, "How many now, Fetch?" And she would call back her count.

At one point, she said, "You might as well put down your gun and come help me—there are so many I can't carry them all back in one trip." I knew we were in trouble! I didn't know how many we had, but it was obvious we had more than we were supposed to have, and it was only 7:05 am—barely sunrise.

We started our harvest, and when we were finished, we had eighteen bluebills in the blind. Well, not exactly. Since we were in a marsh blind and knew that "the man" could easily check on us if he wanted to, we had 14 ducks proudly displayed in the blind and four secretly hidden far back in the tall sawgrass behind the blind. It would have taken a hungry coon to find those four "over the limit" bluebills.

Obviously, we couldn't do any more shooting. I told "Fetch" that I was going to take a walk in the marsh because I knew James would not be back before 9 or 10 o'clock.

When I got back, "Fetch" was nowhere to be found. I didn't worry too much at that point because I figured she had just decided to take a little walk of her own. It was a beautiful morning, and there are all kinds of interesting things to find in the marshes around Cedar Island.

After a while, I did become a little concerned because I could not see her anywhere. So I began to call. Normal voice at first, and then pretty loudly.

Remember how thick I told you the sawgrass is. Well, the sun was fully up, and the day was warming up nicely. After calling for a while, I noticed a large clump of sawgrass behind the blind begin to move, and there was no wind blowing. Slowly, "Fetch" got up, yawned and stretched, and said, "Is something wrong?"

With the sun beating down and warmly dressed in about 25 pounds of down, "Fetch" had curled up in the sawgrass, which was so thick it would easily support a person's body weight, and had taken a long winter's nap.

And why not? Her day had been made! Eighteen bluebills in 35 minutes!

When James came, we explained our predicament about the "over the limit" birds, and he said not to worry, that he had his license, and we could take them all in—if we didn't want them, the motel would cook them up with rutabagas (turnips to "city folks") and make stews out of them. Well, needless to say, we kept the ducks and enjoyed a nice ride back to the port for an earlier than planned trip home—with a very satisfying feeling of a "good hunt" behind us and very confident in "Fetch's" retrieving abilities.

Horace, Do You Like Clams?

Now how does any sane person answer that question? Of course I love clams. I didn't know the significance of my reply when Dallas Goodwin asked me the question one day on the way in from hunting. After he had asked it, I sort of dismissed it from my mind.

We finished our hunt that particular trip, and on the last day, Dallas said, "What time are you leaving in the morning?" I told him that we would probably leave about 9:00 am since we were in no big hurry to get home. Dallas said that was good and asked if I would stop by the dock before leaving the island—he had something he wanted me to take home. I said, "Sure I could."

The next morning, we went about the business of packing up, having a light breakfast, checking out, and heading down to the dock on the way off the island. As we pulled up, Dallas was just returning from depositing his morning load of hunters. When he saw me, he motioned me over to the fish house. The fish house is at the end of the dock, and it is one of many off-loading places for fish catches during the season. Nothing was in season right now except clamming, which could only be done three days a week by law. We walked into the fish house, and Dallas handed me a sack of clams that I could not lift by myself.

He said, "Here, these are the chowder-type clams we catch here. Hope you enjoy them." Of course, he wouldn't dream of letting me pay for these clams, even though I offered. He had gone out on his own the previous day and dredged these up just for us to enjoy as a way of saying, "You're okay, and I want to do something nice for you."

Clam sacks at Cedar Island hold about 250 LARGE chowder clams, and it took Charlene about four or five days of constant dropping them in boiling water to open them up, then taking out the large clams, chopping them up, and freezing them for chowder later on. We had enough clams for clam chowder for a year. We gave a lot of them away to our friends—after all, where are you going to be able to get fresh clams right out of the sound for your own personal clam chowder? Needless to say, they were outstanding, and I will ever be indebted to Dallas for his kindness, hard work, and generosity. Just another example of the type of people who live and work at Cedar Island—can't beat them!

Would You Like to Take Home a Few Oysters?

Are you kidding? I love oysters better than clams!

One night, Jerry said, "Are you going to be here on Friday night? We are going to have an oyster roast!" Unfortunately, I had to decline because I had some business trip to make and had to go home before Friday. I was really upset, because I had heard about Cedar Island oyster roasts but had never been there when they were having one.

Occasionally, Jerry will plan a buffet meal for his hunters, and believe it or not, these are even better than ordering from the menu, if that is possible. They will fix fresh duck, fish of all kinds, all the raw and roasted oysters you can eat, corn, potatoes, fresh collard greens (and when you eat Marcel's fresh collard greens, you will swear that you have died and gone to heaven), turkey and dressing, green beans, several types of salads and cole slaw, and absolutely the best crab casserole you ever put a fork into, with fresh lemon pie for dessert. Ooo—whee! What a treat!

Anyway, I was feeling a little sorry for myself since I was going to miss the oyster roast. On our last night, Jerry said, "Would you like to take some oysters home with you since you can't stay for the roast?" Naturally, I said that I would love to, if he had enough to share some. He told me to pull my truck up to the back of the kitchen and bring my cooler. I backed up and opened my 86 quart Igloo. Jerry started shoveling oysters into the cooler. I started to stop him when it was about half full, but he insisted on filling it up. I have no idea how many oysters I brought home, but we had oyster stew for months.

Before I left, he asked me if I knew the trick of opening them up, and I had to admit that I didn't. He said,

"Wait a minute and I'll show you." He returned with an oyster knife and showed me how and then watched me open a few to make sure I understood how.

When I got home, I sat in front of the TV watching New Year's Day football games and shucking oysters. After that cooler full, I felt like a bonafide oyster shucker and could compete with about anyone. I didn't stick more than eight or ten holes in my hand when the oyster knife slipped, but it is a dull pointed blade, so no permanent damage was done—except to my cholesterol count and my waist line. But it was worth every bite.

Cedar Island Guides Are a Hardy Bunch

As hard as these guys work year around, it is a wonder they live past 35. But maybe that is why they do live so long. However, this little story is not about how hard they work. It is about how they seem to be able to do things that would permanently injure any ordinary person, and it doesn't seem to phase them.

To set the tone for this little tale, you must realize something about these guides. They have to "make do" with what they have. They do not go in for fancy equipment on their boats. Most of them build their own skiffs at considerably below what they would have to pay for a manufactured one. They also outfit them themselves. In fact, the only thing they tend to buy outright from a manufacturer is the motor itself. However, once that motor is installed (again, by them), most of the work that is done on them is performed there on the island by the guides—that is, unless a head has to be replaced or something of a major repair—then it has to be hauled to Morehead City. If you have to make that trip very often, then you will understand why they do most of their work at home.

All this personal work includes the wiring (or the lack of it) that goes into the boat. Even though navigational laws for the state of North Carolina specify red and green bow lights and white stern lights on all boats 14 feet or longer, it is a rare sight to see these types of lights on the fishing boats at Cedar Island. I often wondered why they didn't have them since they run around in the dark at breakneck speeds and can barely see each other. This can present some danger, considering that on a busy morning of duck hunting, as many as six to ten skiffs are leaving the harbor and roaring toward the Banks at about 30 knots—with no lights. Nothing ever seems to happen—no collisions or anything like that, but it is only by the grace of God, I am convinced.

One morning as we left the dock with James, I noticed that he had just installed brand new red and green bow lights, but they were not turned on. I asked him why, and he said that they didn't usually work very well because of the pounding the skiffs took, so he just did not attempt to turn them on unless it was an emergency. I let it go at that, but as I sat under the "house" on the ride out, I couldn't help but wonder how he would turn them on if he had to. I could see some wiring that looked new, but there was no switch in sight.

After we let a group of hunters out, we started off toward the Banks to our blind and curiosity got the better of me. I am a novice boatman, and I pride myself on "perfect" installations of this sort. I was really puzzled about where James had hidden his switch. As we left the marsh blind, I stood up and asked James, "Where is your switch for turning on your bow lights?"

Now James had just finished wading around in the marsh throwing out about 40 decoys, and he was dripping wet. Water literally ran down his hands as he reached under the "house" and casually twisted two live wires together and on came the bow lights. He said, "How do you like my switch? That's why I don't use it more often, because the dumb wires don't seem to want to stay together with all this bouncing around."

I was incredulous. If I had tried that, I would have been electrocuted—no doubt in my mind, yet it seemed perfectly natural to James.

Although I trust James explicitly to put me onto ducks, to find me in the dead of dark in the remotest blind, and to always be there when he is needed, I am not sure that I would want him to "wire" my next boat—he could build it, because it would be done right—but wire it, thanks just the same!

If You Need a Kidney Workout, go to Cedar Island

I have been hunting in four-wheel vehicles over terrain a mountain goat would have difficulty negotiating, but I have never had rougher rides than I have had in skiffs at Cedar Island.

The average depth of Core Sound is probably not more than six to eight feet. This is one of the reasons that the flat-bottomed skiffs are so popular there. It allows the crab fishermen to get in and out of shallow coves and cuts in the marsh that V-bottom hulls simply could not negotiate.

There is a problem with the flat-bottomed skiffs. When the weather is calm, the ride is pleasant—but when the weather turns foul, nothing will jar your brains like a flat-bottomed boat trying to negotiate four to six foot seas.

We learned a trick early on. The first thing you do upon entering the boat in the morning for the ride out, and in the evening for the ride in, is to grab a life jacket. No, not for the reasons you are thinking. It is to sit on to protect your butt from bouncing a foot or so in the air and coming back down on that hard plank you sit on. Another trick we learned is to ride on the port side going out and on the starboard side coming back. I am not exactly sure why, but it was a tip from Dallas, and it really works. It is a much smoother ride for some reason.

While the life jacket is a great idea, if you are riding in a boat with one of the "houses" on the front, there is not much clearance from your head to the roof. If you are not careful, when you hit a large wave head-on, you will crack your head on the roof and bust your "arse" on the way down—a most uncomfortable ride to be sure. The secret is to sit on the life jacket and then hold onto the underside of the seat with your hands. If it is really rough, and you cannot stand up, which helps immensely, then squat in the middle of the boat so that your knees absorb the shock of the waves.

One final tip—if it is a rough day, use the potty in the blind (or in the case of men, outside the blind) just before boarding the boat for the trip home. Man, let me tell you—if you get into that boat in rough seas having to go to the bathroom and are bounced all over that skiff for the 30 to 40 minute ride home—well, you just don't know misery until you have been in that situation; and believe me, it is a situation you want to avoid at all costs.

If you don't have strong kidneys, or if you believe this is a bunch of bunk, I suggest you opt for a close-in marsh blind and not go to the Banks if the weather is rough.

At Cedar Island, Sharp Curves Mean SHARP CURVES

The first time Charlie and I ever went to Cedar Island was almost our last.

In those days, I had a 1979 Lincoln Town Car—a real barge, but a fine road car. We were loaded to the gills, so the car was a little "rear-end heavy."

We had made the twisty road from Morehead City without incident and were approaching the island itself. Just before you enter the Cedar Island community proper (you have already crossed the bridge to the island), there is a straight stretch of a couple of miles through marshlands with small canals on either side of the road. Just before you come into the part of the island that is inhabited, there is a sign that says 20 MPH, indicating a sharp curve.

I suppose that I was doing about 50 or 60 as I approached the curve, but I assumed that if it said 20 MPH, it really meant that you could probably take it about 40 or 50 MPH with little difficulty. I let off the accelerator, but I don't believe I touched the brakes. I started into the curve and pretty quickly realized there was no way to hold the car on my side of the road. I was afraid to hit the brakes hard because American cars then, particularly battleships like this big Lincoln, were not designed with suspension systems to handle these types of curves at this speed. I could sense Charlie tensing up, and to make matters worse, neither of us had our seatbelts on—being the "macho" men that we were (more like "stupid" men upon reflection).

As the headlights hit the curve, I was convinced no good was going to come of this experience. The only choice I had was to "go with the flow" and take the entire road.

As we went into the first part of the curve, I just let the car have its way and turned the wheels as much as I dared. Tires squealing, we made the first bend and then headed straight through the curve to the other side of the road—and directly toward the woods and water beyond the edge of the road.

Applying some brake pressure now, and holding onto the steering wheel for dear life, we skidded around the curve by going across the opposite lane, onto the shoulder about two feet from the water, and then, by applying gas, careened on around the curve. If anyone had been coming down the other side, an accident would have been unavoidable.

We had to stop the car on the side of the road for a few minutes just to catch our breath. Now when I go to Cedar Island, if it says 20 MPH, I do it in 10. No sense in ruining a perfectly good hunt because of stupidity. By the way, Charlie and I now wear our seatbelts all the time. No more "macho" for me!

Game Wardens Have Their Ways

Fred Collins is a frequent hunter at Cedar Island. I do not know Fred very well, but he seems like an okay guy.

This year, Fred brought his boys with him, and I suspect that they all learned a very valuable lesson.

This was the day that the game warden was checking up on people and passed us by with me in the blind with an unplugged gun. We were lucky, but one of Fred's boys wasn't so lucky.

It was a slow day by anybody's standards. Charlie and I had done okay, but it was because Howard Gaskill, our new guide, had seemed to put us into one of the best blinds on the sound. Fred and his boys were hunting several miles north of us—the direction the game warden went after coming so close to checking up on us.

About two o'clock, when Howard came to check on us, he told us that the warden had ticketed one of Fred's sons, but he did not know what the offense was. To my knowledge, no one at Jerry's had ever been ticketed before, so this was a new experience for all of us. There are other hunting outfits along the Crystal Coast, particularly down at Davis and Atlantic, and it is not uncommon to hear that some of those hunters have been ticketed. I don't know what they do down there, but I understand that most of the offenses are for baited blinds. Jerry and the guides at Cedar Island do bait blinds before the season, but I have no proof that they do it illegally after the season begins. Apparently, "anything goes" at Davis and Atlantic, because we hear of hunter offenses all the time down there.

Well, naturally our curiosity was high as we came in that day wondering what Fred's son had done.

The story is that they got bored and unloaded on a sea gull. Unfortunately, as it turns out, they shot the sea gull as the warden was heading their way from our area. As he rode by, he saw the sea gull in the water and judged from the direction in which it was floating that it must have come from Fred's son's blind. He picked up the sea gull and went straight to their blind. When he questioned them if they had shot the gull, they denied it—knowing that the penalty could be very stiff if they admitted to shooting an illegal quarry.

Then the game warden took out a thermometer and took the gull's temperature and explained to the boys that the gull had to have been shot within the past five minutes, and would they care to change their story because the bird had to have been shot from their blind. I supposed they realized they would be only compounding their problems by continuing to deny it, so they admitted their transgression.

Actually, they got off pretty lucky. They were fined $100 but were allowed to keep their guns and licenses, and to continue hunting. Now there is a game warden who got up on the "right" side of the bed that morning, because it could have really gone badly for them.

That night at dinner, Fred was telling the story and told everyone that his son was going to pay his own fine—I think Fred Collins' sons learned a valuable lesson about boredom on that trip.

Other Sights and Sounds to Keep You Awake

Occasionally, it does get a little boring in the blind when nothing is flying. There are walking trips you can take, and you can always wade out and rearrange your decoy set—it probably doesn't do any good, but it makes you feel like you are doing something.

Cedar Island is not far from Cherry Point Marine Air Base and Seymour Johnson Air Force Base in Goldsboro. If you get bored, just look up in the sky, and on most any given day, you can witness practice dog fights from the fly-boys at these bases.

Sometimes they will buzz the sound, and it is a pretty sight to see. I used to get upset when they would come down low until I realized that sometimes this flushes ducks sitting in the marshes on the Banks, and maybe the pilots know we are having a slow day and are trying to help us out.

During the last couple of years, Charlie and I have watched training exercises with a tanker refilling helicopters. They fly back and forth about a half mile above us practicing their routine.

It's not shooting ducks, but it is a fun past-time when the only things flying are sea gulls and shore birds.

We appreciate the boys from Cherry Point and Seymour Johnson—they have given us some pleasant entertainment during the brief boring periods that can be experienced at Cedar Island.

If You Don't Grab That Wand—Boy, It Will Kill You!

About 1980 or so, I thought I was going to get into camping in a big way, so I bought a "cab over camper" on the bed of a 1978 Chevrolet truck. This monster had a 454 engine in it, and carrying all that weight around, we were lucky to get about six or seven miles to the gallon. Nevertheless, most of the time, it ran pretty good, and Charlie and I took trips to Canada and New Mexico before it gave up the ghost.

The old truck was hardly ever used except for these long junkets, and it seemed that every time I cranked it up to go somewhere, some little thing would be wrong with it. Probably just because it was driven so infrequently.

Therefore, to try and keep it in decent shape, I decided to start taking it to the coast on our hunting trips.

I have always been a stickler for taking care of my "stuff" because I knew that if I didn't, it wouldn't work properly when I needed it. For that reason, whenever I went to the coast duck hunting, I would always detour back through Beaufort instead of taking the short cut because there was a big drive-through car wash that could handle that big camper, and I would wash it down thoroughly. Even though I never went anywhere near sand on these trips to duck hunt, I still fastidiously washed that truck all over, even underneath, before the trip home.

On this occasion, Charlie was sick as a dog. Probably ate one too many of Jerry's pimento cheese sandwiches. Whatever the reason, he was "green" and hardly felt like sitting up in the truck, much less driving any. He managed to keep going while we were hunting, but when we started home, he just let go and was really a basket case by the time we left Cedar Island.

I knew he was anxious to get on home, and it was about a six-hour drive, so I asked him if he minded if we stopped in Beaufort so I could wash the truck. Of course, he said that was fine.

It was a bitter cold day, as I recall, when we pulled into the car wash at Beaufort. Charlie stayed in the truck because he would have been no use to anyone in his condition.

In those days, the car washes were not as sophisticated as they are today, and all they had were wands that shot water out at a velocity that would almost take the paint off your car. No brushes and no multi-speed wands like they have today.

I got out, grabbed the wand, pumped in two quarters, and began to wash down the truck. Somewhere in the process, I put the wand down and put my foot on it so it wouldn't squirt away from me so I could straighten a mirror on the truck. As I leaned over to straighten the mirror, I lost my "footing" on the wand, and it slipped out from under my foot.

With the water pressure coming out of that wand at the speed of light, and the velocity similar to that of a cannon, it began to fly all around the washing stall. It banged against the truck and off the wall, and it sprayed me, the stall, and the truck indiscriminately. It was like a huge snake gone berserk. Charlie, despite his feeling rotten, was doubled over in the truck howling with laughter as I valiantly chased this stupid wand all around the stall.

By the time I got it under control, everything within a half mile of the car wash was soaked, including me. I was mad as hell, but Charlie was having such a good time at my expense that I forgot about my stupidity for a few moments and had a good laugh with him.

The only good that came out of this experience is that it seemed to take Charlie's mind off of how he felt for a few hours and made the trip home a little more pleasant for him. I guess that made it worth my getting thoroughly soaked in the "battle of the car wash."

A Breeding Ground for Commerce

I have already alluded to the fact that sometimes it gets a bit boring in the blind during the middle of the day when all the birds seem to settle down for a little siesta. This is when you straighten decoys, take walks to the Banks, take naps, eat, and generally invent ingenious ideas for improving your success as duck hunters.

Charlie has a phrase that he has used ever since I have known him, and it goes something like this, "If a fella had this…" or "If a fella had that…he could do thus and so." When I hear that phrase, I perk up my ears because I know that some wild and clever scheme is about to be brewed.

We have thought up a few hairbrained ideas during lulls at Cedar Island, and here are some of them.

The Radio-Controlled Decoy! Often, ducks will sit in flocks just out of gun range and taunt you all day. Buffleheads are notorious for this kind of behavior. They seem to know just how much they can get away with without coming close enough to be shot at. We figured, "If a fella had himself…a radio-controlled decoy with a powerful motor to ride the waves, we could send that decoy over to those sitting ducks and spook them into flight." We could easily control it from the blind, and we could maneuver it in and out of the sitting ducks until they got tired of being interfered with, and they would get up and fly—maybe toward us. Who knows, it might work.

The Break-Down .22 Rifle! This is another one of our ideas to get those out-of-range sitting ducks moving. Now, we are not proposing something that is illegal.

We don't want to actually shoot ducks with the .22, we just thought it would be neat to carry one of the break-down models along to the blind, and when we saw some ducks sitting 300 or 400 yards away, pop a few shots over their way to spook them up into the air. Sounds reasonable, doesn't it?

The Audible Radar! "If a fella had himself...a small, portable, battery-powered radar screen that could be set up in the blind that would scan about 300 to 400 yards out and pick up any flying activity with a body temperature in excess of 70° and then "beep" when something was spotted, you could quickly wake up from your nap, check the screen, and see some "blips" were coming at you from a certain direction. Then you would be wide awake and ready when they arrived.

Not only would this put a cease to the ducks that sneak by you, but it would solve the severe cases of "crack-eye" that everyone gets from looking through those slits all day long into the wind. What do you think?

The Sea-Colored Retrieving Raft! A lot of times when the wind is blowing hard, a downed duck can actually drift faster than you can walk. Also, sometimes the water can get too deep for you to wade as you go away from the blind trying to retrieve a duck. I have seen many situations where you simply have to let a perfectly good duck drift away because you either cannot make enough speed in your waders to catch it or the water gets too deep to negotiate.

What if you had a one-man, sea-colored (so the ducks wouldn't be spooked by it under your blind) rubber raft that you could tie to the blind. Then when a duck goes down a long way from the blind, you could jump into your raft and paddle out to it faster than you can walk. Then you could just use the rope to pull yourself back to the blind, or you could paddle back. I suppose a small, 4.5 horsepower motor on the back would make the process even easier, but the weight of carrying that motor to the blind might be more trouble than it is worth. However, the boat idea is feasible because it could be inflatable, and the paddle could be collapsible. So you could easily transport the whole rig in a small bag and then inflate it when you got into the blind. It would be ready for the day's work. Huh?

The 70 MM Howitzer! In the days of the "clouds of ducks," which unfortunately you don't see so much of anymore, we kept wondering how we could bring down more ducks—particularly the high fliers.

I know you are supposed to pick out a single duck to shoot at, and if he falls, then pick out another and shoot at it. That's what the experts tell you. But when literally thousands of ducks are flying over your head at about 20 to 30 yards away (and that's the way it used to be), how in the world can you pick out a single duck? You just cannot do it, and anyone who tells you they do, I am not sure I'd buy a used car from them.

What you end up doing is "flock shooting." You simply cannot help it no matter how hard you try. Now flock shooting is not all bad. When the ducks are that thick, it is almost impossible to miss. I have seen two and sometimes three ducks drop with a single shot when the flocks are that thick. Of course, these are not clean kills, and you may have to finish them off in the water as you wade, but you get them down, and they are retrievable.

But—"What if a fella had…a 70 millimeter Howitzer with the shell loaded with about 80,000 BBs that you could fire into those thousands of ducks?"

Can you imagine, hundreds would be lying all over the water around your blind, and you would need a net and two boats to pick all of them up. Of course, this would be illegal, and we know that, but it's fun to fantasize sometimes, isn't it?

M R Duks

About 1982 or 1983, Charlene and I were at Cedar Island, and even though we had been going for several years, we were still something of novices.

One morning, we came in to breakfast. We were running a little late that morning, so we did not get our customary table near the buffet tables. Therefore, when the food came out, several people jumped up ahead of us and beat us to the punch.

As we stood in line, I noticed a handwritten sign posted above the buffet table that read like this:

C M DUKS
M R NOT DUKS
OSAR
C M WANGS–
L I B
M R DUKS

I puzzled over this sign for a while but could not figure it out. At first I thought, "I wonder if these are some new guides and Jerry has put their names up so we will recognize them?" Mr. C. M. Duks, Mr. C. M. Wangs, surely Mr. Osar was Oscar, and I supposed L. I. B. could be someone who just goes by his initials. Was M. R. Duks also new, and who could Mr. M. R. Not Duks be? That last one didn't make any sense at all.

I pointed it out to Charlene, and she was having the same difficulty as I was in trying to make sense out of it. Jerry came up and said, "Do you understand my sign?" He had a sheepish grin on his face, and I was not about to tell him my theory. The safest bet was simply to admit that I did not know what it meant. He said, let me read it to you, and then see if it makes sense. What he read sounded something like this:

    See 'em ducks?
    'Em are not ducks!
    Oh es they are.
    See 'em wings?
    Ell I be,
    'Em are ducks!

    We got a big laugh out of that and really felt quite dumb not being able to figure it out for ourselves.

    We were so impressed by this little poem that Charlene cross-stitched it for Jerry and presented it to him the next year. It now hangs proudly in the restaurant for all the incoming hunters to see—and to try and figure out.

Christmas at Cedar Island

Opening day of the duck hunting season is usually around the middle of December, and one of the reasons we always like to be there is not just for the excitement of the hunt, but by that time, Cedar Island is decked out for Christmas.

Christmas is a really big occasion for Cedar Island people. They go all out in decorating their homes. If you are privileged to go into one of their homes, you will likely see one of the prettiest Christmas trees you have ever witnessed.

There is a bend in the road as you go by the old oyster processing plant near one of the bridges that boasts one of the most beautifully decorated homes on the island. You have to look to your left just as you are going around the curve and look out over the water to the opposite bank to see it. It is a white, two-story house with black trim, and the decorations on this house are just stunning. They reflect off the water, and it serves as our introduction to Cedar Island Christmas time.

As you progress further into the inhabited part of the island, one of the first houses you pass is Jerry Gaskill's on the right. You can always tell Jerry's house because of the garland wrapped around the two entrance poles at the front of his driveway.

As you get closer to the motel, if you know just where to look at just the right time, you can spot James' new home tucked back in the pine trees off to the left. It is decorated all over with hundreds of feet of stringed lights.

All the houses on the island are similarly decorated, and it really puts you in the Christmas mood—if you are not already in it before you get there.

They go all out at the motel too. The tree is always beautiful, and the restaurant is appropriately decorated with wreaths, holly, and all the trimmings. Although I have never actually spent a Christmas at Cedar Island, I would like to one day—it promises to be an experience I will likely not forget for a long time.

The Exploding Beanee Weanees

Have you ever wondered what you would smell like if you had been soaked in Beanee Weanees and had to sit in a duck blind all day with no way to wash them off? Probably not, but I can tell you it is not the most pleasant experience.

Remember how you can heat things up by putting them on top of the Coleman heater, and then when you put the lid over them, it acts like an oven? Well, Charlie and I had the bright idea one day that "hot" Beanee Weanees would certainly taste better than cold ones. Cold is okay, but when it is about 20° outside and the wind chill is down to about 20° below zero, hot Beanee Weanees just sounded better.

Since everything else worked so well with the stove concept, why not the Beanee Weanees?

So on they went. We realized that it would probably take several minutes to heat up a cold can of beans, so we sort of forgot about them. One nice thing about heating up Wranglers is that you can smell them when they begin to get hot, and you know it is about time to take them off the "cooker." What we soon realized is that you cannot smell a can of Beanee Weanees cooking, particularly if the lid is still fastened on tight.

Well, it didn't take long for us to "smell" them and "wear them" at about the same instant.

About fifteen minutes after putting the can on the cooker, there was a resounding explosion in the blind. The top of the cooker flew up about two feet, and Beanee Weanees flew all over us and the blind. At first I thought that Charlie had shot at a duck, but when he didn't get up, I knew it could not have been that. Then I thought maybe he had shot himself in the foot out of boredom, but Charlie is not that stupid. It did not take long to figure out what happened as we began to smell the aroma of hot Beanee Weanees—all over us, our gear, and the inside of the blind. In fact, we had just redecorated our blind in a brown ooze that only an exploding can of Beanee Weanees can make.

The moral of this story is simple. If you don't want to have to explain to your guide and your hunting companions why you smell like a Beanee Weanee factory at the end of the day, if you are going to heat up a can of "anything" using our "stove method," I suggest you slightly open the lid of the can you are heating to allow a little pressure to escape while your feast is heating.

We learned the hard way—now you don't have to!

There Is More to Cedar Island Than Just Killing Ducks

I am always amazed every time I go to Cedar Island to hear the griping, complaining, and bitching of some of the hunters who go there because they did not see many ducks that day. To listen to them, if you pay about $100 a day for the hunting trip, you are supposed to be able to shoot every 15 minutes throughout the day.

Speaking of the fee, which is $110 per day, in my judgment, it is the best buy on the east coast. Listen to what you get: your room for the night, the best dinners to be found anywhere, a complete breakfast with everything imaginable and all you can eat, a good packed lunch to carry with you, guide fees, boat transportation, a couple of checks per day by the guide, and a 40 to 60 decoy spread put out and picked up by the guides. Now, I ask you, where can you beat all of that for $110 a day? And I haven't even begun to discuss Cedar Island's greatest assets, its people.

Before I talk about all the advantages of Cedar Island, I need to comment on this "killing mania" I hear so much about from disgruntled hunters. I am going to be blatantly honest with you: I have made about 100 trips to Cedar Island to hunt, and I can count on the fingers of one hand the days I did not get my limit. Yes, we have had some bluebird days, but not many. And even on those days when the ducks didn't fly as often as we would have liked, by staying alert, we have still managed to get our limits most days.

What I think happens is one of two things: either these people are not very good shots and miss more than they are willing to admit to or, when the activity isn't fast and furious, they get lulled into complacency and miss many opportunities to shoot because they are not alert.

There have been countless times when I have looked all around the blind, using the slits to see if anything was coming so I could get up and stretch, and not seeing anything, I would get up, and not 30 seconds later, a small flock would buzz by me that I never saw coming while I was looking around.

My point is that when you get lazy, opportunities literally fly by you that many of these people probably never see—and then they come in complaining that "there are no ducks at Cedar Island!" Bullshit, they are there—you just have to be diligent in looking for them and not let your guard down.

I don't go to Cedar Island just to kill ducks. I could do that at home on our lakes, rivers, and ponds. There are many reasons I go, and here are a few of them.

As strange as it sounds, I enjoy the preparation, anticipation, and the trip down there just about as much as the hunting itself. Just thinking about the scenery, the food, the friendships, the stop at Neuse Sporting Goods, eating at King's, and just the ride through the marshlands, and finally, crossing the bridge to Cedar Island, the memories flood through your mind as you approach one of your favorite places on earth.

The people, the people, and the people! Jerry and Charran are the greatest hosts in the world. They go out of their way to make sure that "every" guest is treated marvelously. They will do anything to make sure your accommodations are fine and that you have everything you need for a successful and enjoyable trip.

The guides! They work harder than anyone I know to ensure a good hunt. They will move you without complaining if you request it—and sometimes they take the initiative themselves if they believe you will get better shooting somewhere else.

Marcel! The best cook on the east coast. What else do you need to know?

Martha Day, Monique, and the other waitresses! They work their buns off to make sure you get served promptly and courteously whenever you are in the dining room.

The scenery! Have you ever been in a skiff roaring across the bays and sounds toward the Outer Banks at dawn with barely enough light to see where you are going? Wind is blowing in your face and blinds and marshes are barely discernible in the predawn twilight—no feeling like it in the world. Sitting in a blind near the Banks as the sun creeps up over the horizon and the marshes and bays come to life with waterfowl. Huge flocks soar overhead, leaving their nightly nests off to a day of feeding—swooping near your blind as you prepare to shoot. Watching the sun come up and illuminate your decoy spread as another exciting day begins. Then, later in the afternoon, as you wait to be picked up, you are greeted with one of the most gorgeous sunsets you can imagine as the pink and red rays stretch out over miles of bays, sounds, and marshes. Finally, the ride home where you can now easily see the dotted islands of Core Sound and the marshes as you head to port (all the time thinking, "How in the world do these guides know where they are going in the morning when you can barely see 20 yards in front of you?").

And not to be underestimated is the feeling of pleasant exhaustion as you reach the room, come out of all those clothes, and stand under a hot shower anticipating dinner.

Oh yes, there are many reasons to go to Cedar Island, and shooting ducks is only one small part of it. If I didn't get a single duck, it is still a bargain, and I would do it over and over again.

About the Author

Horace Oden Kelly, Jr.
June 28, 1938–February 6, 1996

Horace O. Kelly, Jr. lived life to the fullest and accomplished a great deal in his short time on earth. Born and raised in Nashville, TN, the only son of Horace O. Kelly, Sr. and Chettie Mae Kelly, he received his BA and MA in psychology from Baylor University, while there on scholarship for both baseball and basketball, and his PhD from Kennedy-Western University.

He spent most of his career in marketing research for several companies, including Coca-Cola in Atlanta, GA, British Petroleum in Cleveland, OH, and R.J. Reynolds Tobacco Company in Winston-Salem, NC. In 1975, he founded Horace Kelly and Associates, the first independent marketing research firm in Winston-Salem. By 1980, his company focused on agriculture and became the first company in the United States to specialize in agricultural chemical marketing research.

He began lecturing at Wake Forest University in 1986 and found a love for teaching, which led to selling his company and joining the faculty of the business school as a professor of strategic management and entrepreneurship. In 1994, he was named assistant dean of the Wayne Calloway School of Business and Accountancy at Wake Forest University.

Horace O. Kelly, Jr. was passionate about family, teaching, golf, fishing, and hunting. He immortalized his memories and life lessons learned from his time duck hunting in his book, Cedar Island Duck Hunting Experiences.

About the Republication of Cedar Island Duck Hunting Experiences

My father self-published his duck hunting memoir in 1990, which required a one-time printing with a local printer. He sold some through local book stores and at the Driftwood Motel in Cedar Island, but he found the most joy from giving the books away as gifts to friends, family, and colleagues.

I was very close to my father, and his death while I was in college was devastating. I have read this book every few years throughout my life to remember his humor, his kindness, his love of my mother, and his words of wisdom. I've moved from house to house with a box of his books with me through the years and have given them away from time to time. I gave copies away at my wedding as a way to remember him on a day he couldn't be there.

As the supply of books has gotten smaller and I talk to my children more about their grandfather, I realized I wanted to share his book and his memory with more people, which is why I decided to republish.

Thank you Lucy Elenbaas for your assistance in editing, and thank you Jessica Cantlin for the beautiful cover photo (feedmywanderlust.com).

Thank you Mom, Omar, Sarah, and Miles.

Lora Kelly Shahine, MD

www.ingramcontent.com/pod-product-compliance
Lightning Source LLC
LaVergne TN
LVHW051101080426
835508LV00019B/1998